How Do You Want Your Room... Plain or Padded?

SANITY-PRESERVING TACTICS FOR TODAY'S WOMAN

Jo Ann Larsen
and Artemus Cole

SHADOW MOUNTAIN
SALT LAKE CITY, UTAH

Quotations from *Cathy* cartoons by Cathy Guisewite reprinted with permission of Universal Press Syndicate.

Quotation from the *Optimist Magazine* reprinted with permission from July 1990 *Reader's Digest* and February 1990 *Optimist Magazine.*

Quotations by Alice Berry, Betty L. Hagerty, Carol Leinen, and Isabel L. Livingstone are reprinted with permission from the January 1981, August 1992, December 1985, and November 1980 issues of the *Reader's Digest,* copyright 1981, 1992, 1985, and 1980 by The Reader's Digest Association, Inc.

Library of Congress Cataloging-in-Publication Data

Larsen, Jo Ann.
   How do you want your room—plain or padded? : sanity-preserving tactics for today's woman / Jo Ann Larsen, Artemus Cole.
      p.   cm.
   ISBN 0-87579-972-8 (pbk.)
   1. Women—Quotations, maxims, etc. 2. Women—Humor.   I. Cole, Artemus. II. Title.
PN6084.W6L37   1995
305.4—dc20   95-19172
                                                                  CIP

Printed in the United States of America   72082

10   9   8   7   6   5   4   3   2

To all the women who are struggling
to keep their lives together in today's world

Jo Ann Larsen and Artemus Cole

Contents

Preface

In today's Western world, most women are soul mates. No matter what their roles—married, single, single parent, or grandparent, worker or homemaker—most are trying to do too much too well. In a day in which many women have added eight or nine hours of work time to their daily schedules without giving up much, and in which even the homemaker's role is ever-changing and sometimes overwhelming, women report that their lives feel chaotic and out of control. There is always something up ahead to do, something behind left undone, and something unraveling. And it feels like their fault.

For a woman, that's when the frustration and the feelings of guilt and inadequacy flood in. She feels discouraged, sometimes even helpless and hopeless. And then, finally, she becomes angry at herself. She's trying as hard and moving as fast as she can—working sometimes sixteen or eighteen hours a day (sometimes with night duty)—and things are still left undone. Even when she's operating at top capacity, she's still not making it. So she often thinks, "There must be something wrong with me. If I just worked harder, organized better, and slept less, I could get things done." Sadly, she concludes that the flaw is in herself, and as a result, she often berates herself endlessly for her inadequacies.

But in the midst of her berating, this woman pauses to ponder her circumstances: "Wait a minute," she says to herself. "I've been working hard all day long, all week long, even all month long—for years and years—so how come it's all my fault I can't keep my act together?" Thinking about the matter logically, she *knows* she can't be completely responsible all the time. Look at how hard she's working, how hard she's pushing nonstop. She feels overburdened, unappreciated, and overworked. It's not fair.

So the woman looks around for another culprit to share the blame, and who does she spy? A husband, if she has one. A husband who isn't helping, or who isn't helping enough. From her perspective, she's out in the lake drowning without a life preserver—going down for the third time— and he's on the shore, wanting his dinner. So now she's angry at him. She wonders why he doesn't rescue her, and this poor, hapless man doesn't even know she's sinking.

"She stayed up all night telling me the things she was going to tell you!"

Other culprits that get press for a woman's life being out of control are her children, if she has any. Maybe it's *their* fault she can't stay afloat, so the woman says things to them like "I do everything for you and you don't appreciate it." Or "You don't care enough about me to clean your room." Or even "You're just like your father." Inadvertently, the woman sometimes puts her children on massive guilt trips—and she's good at it.

One mistake, then, that the '90s woman often makes is in looking for a flaw in herself or someone else. She knows she's having trouble staying afloat, and her conclusion is that it has to be someone's fault. But the truth is, the flaw *isn't* in the woman, or in anyone else, for that matter. The flaw is in a schizophrenic, runaway culture that gives women never-ending conflicting messages about what they should do and be. And because they sometimes fail to filter and choose from these messages, women attempt to respond to many more than is humanly possible. As a result, they reel from stress, often depleting and exhausting themselves and falling into burnout or depression.

Perhaps the most significant factor pressing today's women is the seismic cultural shift in traditional gender roles. Faced in the '90s with financial pressures, dismayed by the high expense of rearing children, and sometimes required to carry on as single parents, women face confusing and confounding choices—wonderful choices, in one respect, that allow for personal growth and development. But choices that also leave a woman staggering because she doesn't know how to meet all her obligations and fulfill all her responsibilities.

In the past, a woman was not expected to take charge of her life. In the '90s, however, she has to. The challenge for today's woman is to become her own taskmaster and guardian, to make her own choices, and to decide on her own priorities. Doing so, however, requires a woman to bring to a conscious level and take control of the implicit cultural messages that drive her to work so hard, to feel so bad, and to expend herself in so many directions.

The six women of the '90s introduced in this book through quotes and through cartoons by Artemus Cole, a veteran national cartoonist, are designed to aid in that challenge. The first five of these women—the caretaker, the juggler, the guilt sponge, the perfectionist, and the pleaser— are actually implicit and runaway cultural themes that we, as women and as creatures of the culture, have absorbed throughout our lives and that unknowingly affect our choices and decisions. These themes, based on culture and tradition though not necessarily on truth, may drive us at an unconscious level to stretch ourselves too far in too many ways.

The sixth woman—the depleted woman—represents the consequences of a woman's not making judicious decisions regarding the expenditure of her time, energy, and resources. Driven by the choices she makes in her caretaking, juggling, pleasing, and perfectionist roles, and by the overwhelming guilt she experiences when she isn't all things to all people, the woman often pushes herself too hard in too many ways and neglects the care of her own self. As you turn the pages of this book, you'll become better acquainted with all six of these women.

The Caretaker

The first woman, the caretaker, is that '90s woman who takes charge of other people's needs and feelings and decisions and who assumes the care and comfort of everyone within her purview. She's the "fix-it" woman who has a twenty-four-hour beeper to alert her to anyone who comes into her space, anyone who may need her help. And she will speed rapidly to meet the needs of that person, sometimes even before he or she has needs.

In the '50s, the caretaker was the woman who, in the main, took emotional responsibility only for her family, and in her role she seriously and carefully managed and kept track of her family, molding her children's behavior within the constricted cultural expectations of the day.

In the '90s, the caretaker is the woman who is still taking emotional responsibility for her family (or, if she's single, for many other people); but in this new world, the number of people she cares for has expanded quantitatively to the point that, as one woman put it, we designate ourselves "general managers of the universe."

"Theodore, put the channel back on PBS."

"There is no end to the people that we take care of," reflects another woman. "When we're through raising our children, then we take care of our grandchildren. And if we're lucky enough, we get to take care of our great-grandchildren." We become, as it were, *veteran* caretakers.

In today's world, as in the '50s, the caretaker's role is the most noble and notable of women's roles, but even that role has to be bounded, because there is no end to the messages bombarding a woman concerning what she ought to do and be. As one woman put it, "For many years, I always felt I was invincible—that I could stretch to take care of as many people, accomplish as many tasks, and borrow from my sleep as much as I wanted, and there would be no penalty. I did that until I burned out and there wasn't enough of *me* left to take care of *them*."

It is, then, the caretaker's challenge to respect the fact that she is finite—that she has limited time, energy, and resources—and that she must respond to the needs of others while staying within her boundaries. This requires that she identify and respond first to her priorities, weeding out of her schedule time-drainers that sap her strength, and that she learn to say no when the occasion merits.

Most caretakers, however, report difficulty in saying no. "If I say no, I might hurt someone," says one. "If I say no, someone will think I'm not doing my job," says another. Still a third says, "I have a 'can do' reputation to protect." Most often the caretaker's difficulty in saying no is consistent with these reasons: she doesn't want to reject anyone and she doesn't want to be rejected or diminished. In her caretaking role, saying no is not a value-neutral issue. Rather, most care-takers emotionalize the issue of saying yes or no, their answers having connotations for their self-esteem and their very viability as human beings.

In that respect, the caretaker's challenge is to approach the issue of saying yes or no as though it were simply a job or a task to be done that needs to be weighed in terms of her priorities, needs, values, interests, time, and resources. The caretaker's bottom line is to reserve the right to priori-tize her life in a way that makes sense to herself without her choices being skewed by whether her worth is at stake.

The caretaker faces another challenge, that of putting her own self on her schedule. The caretaker feels guilty if she's *not* taking care of someone else. And she feels guilty if she *is* taking care of herself. The result is that she often defaults on the care of herself. As one woman puts it: "I would take care of myself, but *they* need me more than *I* need me." Another woman says, "When I think about exercising or practicing my art strokes, I suddenly find myself in the kitchen cooking something wonderful for my husband." A vital issue for each of these women, as with all others, is to keep herself in focus by first, scheduling daily appointments with herself in her day planner for her own care and maintenance, and second, keeping those appointments sacrosanct.

Finally, the caretaker faces the challenge of releasing herself from her house. The word *housewife* means, essentially, a woman "bonded to the house," and indeed, a woman's self-esteem is often bonded or tied up with the condition of her house. If her house is chaotic, she is chaotic.

From the caretaker's perspective, deep down she knows it's *her* job (even when she has help) to keep the house clean (her mother told her so). And if it's not clean, she's flawed. To her, a sock on the floor is a mark on her character. And so she's vulnerable, because in most houses things don't stay put, and in fact, never in recorded history has any woman ever finished the housework. The caretaker's issue, then, is that of protecting her self-esteem by learning to deal with the dirt and clutter in her home without emotionalizing those things.

The caretaker's life is further complicated because very few men make a connection between a sticky floor and a woman's self-worth. He would just like some of her time, please, maybe to sit with him or watch TV, and she declines. "There's work to be done, clutter to clear away, dishes to do, clothes to put away, children to bathe and put to bed, and then I'll relax," she responds.

So then he feels hurt. Housework is more important than his relationship with her. He's taking time out. Why won't she? He gets angry—and shows it. Now she's hurt. She expects him to understand the world the way she does. You *don't* leave dishes!

Here, the conflicts and hurt feelings both sexes feel emanate from the ambiguity of what were once well-defined gender roles. Lacking clear guidelines in the '90s, both sexes need to stop the chore wars and offer the quality of mercy to each other, making a conscious effort to treat housework as simply a task needing to be done, and problem-solving household chores based on available time and resources.

The Juggler

After the caretaker comes the juggler, that hardworking woman who, at home and at work, does an incredible, almost impossible balancing act. This is the busy woman whose every move has to have a work purpose and who prides herself on doing four or five things at a time. And this is the woman who operates from lists—and sometimes, *lists* of her lists. "We have to have lists," says one juggler, "because we have a lot more on our minds than there is room for."

The juggler is also the efficiency expert who's always thinking two or three moves ahead. At work, she eats her lunch while she's preparing her latest report and thinking about her dinner menu for that night or doing leg squats. At home, as she makes sweeps through her house, she's thinking that she'll empty the garbage this time, take a swipe at that cobweb the next trip, and the time after that, she'll pick up the dirty socks.

It is the juggler in the '90s woman who makes it difficult for her to relax. When the juggler stops, she begins to feel somewhere on the scale between "uncomfortable" and "excruciating." "Here I am relaxing," she thinks, "not doing my job." And when she *does* relax, the juggler sometimes does what one woman calls "multiple relaxing": "That's when I sit down and I watch TV and do my nails and sew on buttons and write notes to my friends." But "multiple relaxing," she says, "is really stressful."

*"Goodness, Carol! You tossed and turned all night
worrying about what you're going to do today!"*

In this respect, the juggler's major challenge is to learn to
draw artificial lines that say, "After this time, I don't work. Or
do a particular task or activity. I choose to give myself time
off to take care of myself." It's imperative for the juggler to
establish such artificial lines because there are no instruction
manuals in her world telling her that she can take a break at
two-thirty or that she only has to work until five o'clock. No
one saying, "STOP! You've done enough. You can rest now."
Only the juggler can give herself permission to relax or to
outline the boundaries of her job description.

The juggler also needs to take a deep breath and just *be*
for a while—to learn to live for her todays, to celebrate the
temporary, and to enjoy the fullness and joy of her moment-
by-moment experiencing. And, in the words of Judith Viorst,
the juggler also needs to ponder her priorities, to think
"about what makes us feel good, . . . and what restores our
hurried, harried souls."

As jugglers, Viorst reflects, we can all afford more room
to linger awhile—"to linger over simmering pots and child's
play and talks with friends and music and mending. To savor

the simple acts that give us that sweet sense of peace that I call domestic tranquillity."

The Guilt Sponge

Next comes the guilt sponge, that woman who has guilt festivals about nearly everything nearly all the time. This is the woman who feels guilty when her phone book automatically opens to the pizza parlors. When she's carrying ten extra pounds. Or when the geranium that she got for Mother's Day dies (or she throws it out prematurely).

The guilt sponge is the woman who reels from conflicting "shoulds." Agitating her mind are often hundreds of these "shoulds" that whirl around in her brain, pulling her this way and that, confusing her, and keeping her from feeling good about herself. She should keep her house totally immaculate (all the time), look young and slim and beautiful, exercise every day, feed her kids oatmeal, do the dishes cheerfully, get up earlier. And these "shoulds" that flog a woman's mind are no respecter of how much she is doing, how hard she is trying, or how much she has already accomplished.

The guilt sponge also suffers over things that she can't control, as in the case of a woman who drove by a business every day on her way to work, noticing that the business was failing. One day, she says, as she drove by the business, she saw a "Closed Forever" sign on the door, and the guilt rushed in as she thought, "If I had just frequented that business and if I had just sent my friends in, we might have been able to save it."

One challenge for the guilt sponge is to release herself from feeling responsible for those situations in her life over which she has little or no control. Another challenge is to examine her "shoulds" (and "oughts")—"I should weigh ten pounds less," "I should keep the house mother-clean," "I should always have well-matched children"—and decide whether any of these "shoulds" represent, for her, a true value, a value that is chosen rather than imposed. At issue is a woman's choosing to develop her own mature conscience, a conscience constituted of the behaviors, ethics, values, opinions, preferences that *she* (not someone else) espouses.

Also at issue is a woman's distinguishing between "earned" and "unearned" guilt. At times, guilt is "earned"— that is, a woman has perhaps been unkind or even unforgiving. In such instances, a woman can benefit from apologizing and making amends. But more often, a woman suffers from "unearned" guilt over the many things in her life she takes emotional responsibility for but can't control. In such instances, a woman's challenge is to let go of the unearned guilt and to quit suffering over things she can't change.

The Perfectionist

Following the guilt sponge comes the perfectionist. This is the woman who never has a run in her stocking or a chip in her nails, and whose shoulder pads never slide off her shoulders. This is also the woman whose spices are alphabetically organized. And, as Mary McBride offers, when her children "sit on Santa Claus's lap, they ask for world peace."

The perfectionist is also the woman who sets impossibly high goals for herself and then berates herself endlessly because she can't achieve them. This is the woman who is haunted by her incompletes rather than heartened by her successes, whose achievement is tied closely to her worth. And she is also the woman who doesn't know when to say, "I've done enough. This is good enough."

"No, no, no, Edward! Not the yellow shirt in the red chair!"

The ultimate perfectionist pays a price for her perfectionism in that she fights for her self-esteem every minute of her life because every detail undone accuses her of not doing her job. In that sense, the price she pays is that she is not free; her life is controlled by her list of unaccomplished things. In addition, the perfectionist's drive to achieve imposes high costs to her physical and emotional well-being and may even eventually erode her energy and ability to cope, plunging her into burnout or depression. "No one," in fact, "can do everything and do it well; there is always a price to be paid for doing too much," reflect Claudia Bepko and Jo-Ann Krestan.

Tempering perfectionism is a quest, not an event, for any woman. The perfectionist's challenge is that of releasing herself from having to do *everything* well. In softening her standards and cutting corners, any reforming perfectionist can benefit from the motto, "If it's just barely worth doing, then just barely do it." And from the motto, "Some things are worth doing well. And some things aren't worth doing." And even from the concept of "average"—"I'm going to do just an *average* job of cleaning my house this year." At issue for the perfectionist is examining her production and performance and making informed choices that release her from many of her pressures and burdens.

The Pleaser

After the perfectionist comes the pleaser, the woman who requires the endorsement of others to feel good about herself. If she receives approval from outside sources, the pleaser's self-esteem goes up; if someone disapproves, her self-esteem goes down. In that regard, her very sense of self comes from being valued by or approved of by other people, and any situation that even hints of disapproval can be devastating because it calls her very worth into question.

Among the pleaser's issues are that she sacrifices her own needs in order to please others; that she has difficulty accepting compliments; that another's view of her and her choices is more important than her own; and that she often believes something is inherently wrong with herself. The pleaser also devalues her own opinions and positions, concluding that if her views differ from those of others, she's wrong, and at the extreme, she apologizes excessively for almost everything, including all of her perceived deficiencies.

Complicating the pleaser's vulnerability to the views of others is that she lives in a sea of mood changers in which the emotions and stances of others readily change. In this sense, the pleaser's challenge is to move from an *other-centered* position, which is dependent on validation from the outside world, to a position of *centeredness* and high self-regard in which she is not vulnerable to the capriciousness and whims of people and events over which she has no control.

Becoming centered and achieving that high regard requires that the pleaser view herself as separate from others and realize that anger and disapproval from others has to do with their own issues and choices, not her worth. Others are in charge of their own anger and, in any given instance, will make three basic choices: whether or not to get angry, whether or not to stay angry, and whether or not to express their anger destructively.

When someone exhibits disapproval or is in a bad mood, the pleaser needs to view the problem as residing with the other person. At issue is the pleaser's building a shield around herself, protecting herself from anger or frustration coming her way, leaving it where it belongs—with the other person—and refusing to let it lower her self-esteem.

Also of importance to the pleaser is putting herself in the "I count" position and learning to endorse her own feelings, opinions, and decisions. Coming out into the open and learning to trust her judgment and to depend on herself for accurate information about herself can be an exhilarating experience for a woman, as one woman reflects: "My life changed when I realized there were as many different frames of reference as there are people—and that I was entitled to my *own*."

The Depleted Woman

Finally comes the depleted woman, as represented in one woman's remark that she "didn't do mornings" and another's that "sleeping is the best of two worlds: it allows you to be unconscious and alive at the same time."

Today's depleted woman is that stressed-out woman who eats on the run, who overcommits, who doesn't exercise regularly, who neglects sound nutrition, and who, when she's pushed, chronically borrows from her sleep. Women, in fact, "come up with a thousand reasons why they can't take an hour a day to exercise, meditate, read, soak in the bath, do whatever it is that revitalizes them," reflects an author. (Joseph Procaccini, as quoted by Carol Tannenhauser.)

Inherent in the solutions to the depleted woman's problem is her commitment to establishing a self-repair, maintenance, and enhancement program, which includes all of the regulars—good sleep, sound nutrition, a regular exercise plan, time to relax—and, in addition, preventative health care—health exams and monthly breast self-examinations.

"Is your stress level down enough so that you can start dinner?"

Finally, the depleted woman needs to pay attention to the state of her exhaustion. At times, the depleted woman falls into an actual clinical depression, in which all the lifestyle changes in the world can't break the hold of the hopelessness and despair that set in. There is a stark difference between depression-the-blues, which can affect any woman periodically, and depression-the-chemical-disorder, which is a physical, sometimes even genetic illness, akin to ulcers or high blood pressure, triggered by a change in the chemicals in the brain.

In cases in which a woman experiences over time such symptoms of depression as sleep disturbance, difficulty concentrating, a low energy level, rapid mood swings, low stress tolerance, loss of appetite, or withdrawal or isolation from friends or family, she may need to obtain medical treatment for her disorder. As one psychiatrist stresses, "People don't realize there is a difference between the mind and the brain. The mind is what we think of as ourselves, and the brain is an organ. When a person suffers from a chemical depression, the brain's chemicals are imbalanced, and in such instances the brain, as an organ, needs medications just as the liver, heart, or lung needs treatment when there is a problem with them." (Susan Mirow.)

Other Issues

Of issue to all the '90s women—the caretaker, the juggler, the guilt sponge, the perfectionist, the pleaser, and the depleted woman—is recognizing that taking today's cultural roller coaster ride is a choice. Each of these women is represented in unconscious, embedded, cultural aspects of ourselves that we as women can become aware of and substantially bring under control. We do not *have to* let these driving forces determine our choices, aggravate our guilt, and lower our self-esteem. Nor do we need to let them cause our burnout and depression.

As '90s women, we are pioneers who must carve out new roles under unprecedented conditions. Yet we are using many outmoded remnants of cultural programming from the past to analyze and assess our adequacy in the present. Our most basic challenge as today's women is designing a set of guidelines for performance and assessment that work in a new world in which we ourselves can be a relevant guiding force in assessing our priorities. Other guiding forces—our religious background and our current family situation, for instance—help us set priorities. But it's up to us to make wise decisions regarding how to spend our time and energy.

At issue first, if you are like most women, is taking better care of yourself—making decisions about your life care and your lifestyle having to do with eating and exercise and sleep that improve your emotional and physical well-being. At issue, second, is realizing that you're in charge of your own choices and the number of commitments you make. It's as vital to budget your time, energy, and resources as it is to budget your money.

"I'll never understand why she waits till the last minute!"

One option in budgeting and gaining control of your time expenditures is to put a category on your schedule in your day planner for the care and maintenance of yourself and then a category for the important people in your life. Fund these categories with time allotments and, after that, categorize and fund the other important causes and commitments in your life. Next, decide how to allocate other time to other, less important causes. Grant yourself the right to determine your own boundaries and the right to preserve your resources for those tasks and people that you yourself prioritize.

At issue, finally, in the '90s are the challenges embodied in a woman's accepting her own appearance and investing in herself as a maturing human being. In the later chapters of this book, I've addressed these subjects, along with women's health. As with the culturally specific attributes embodied in each of the six women of the '90s, today's woman also receives conflicting and confusing cultural messages about her appearance and body image. For most women, appearance is a continual problem. They feel that their bodies are not good enough, pretty enough, thin enough, firm enough, or young enough, and they couple their appearance with their own worth.

One challenge in coming to terms with your appearance and body image is remembering that beauty is a culturally defined trait that has varying and, most times, contradictory facets that no one woman can achieve. Inherent in this challenge is the task of releasing yourself from having to achieve any particular model. Enhance your appearance to the extent *you'd* like—but don't try to achieve an ideal set by someone else or by any of the anonymous *theys* of this world.

Another challenge is giving yourself permission to have body flaws. "If we saw the same models that appear in *Vogue* in the grocery store without their makeup and all their trappings, they would look just like us," says one woman. It is through the use of makeup artists, creative lighting, and sensitive camera lenses that the media models present an inflated norm against which the average woman can't compete.

Finally, give yourself the latitude to be comfortable with your own weight. "In the back of every woman's mind is the thought, 'I have to lose ten pounds,'" says one woman. "And when each of us dies, on her lips will probably still be the indictment, 'I didn't lose ten pounds.'" As an option to suffering over your body weight, consider what weight is really realistic for you to achieve, follow through on a goal to achieve it, and then give yourself permission to be at that weight without self-recrimination.

The final challenge for the '90s woman is to invest in herself as a forever-growing human being and to take full responsibility for her own growth and maintenance. "People often say that this or that person has not yet found [herself]," reflects Thomas Azasz. "But the self is not something that one finds. It is something that one creates."

For a woman, defining or even enhancing a self requires certain core conditions: First, recognizing that she is an intrinsically valuable human being deserving of her own investment. Second, acting to find interests and activities of her own that she takes initiative to pursue, even when there are pulls from outside forces to dissuade her from continuing her investments. Third, viewing herself as an ever-evolving human being, capable of continuing growth and maturity through all the seasons of her life.

As with all other challenges in the '90s, in a growth process a woman's task is to take responsibility for herself as her own taskmaster and guardian. It is the woman who feels good about herself and her life, and who reaches to meet her own as well as others' needs, who is able to give fully to herself and those she loves.

In this book you'll read comments and quotes from women and about women. Some of these quotes are taken from the helpful books and articles listed at the end of this book. Others are the comments of the hundreds of women I have met, counseled, or spoken to at seminars through the years.

Chapter 1

Today's Woman

In the '90s, many women are straddling the office and the home front, adding the role of perfect worker in the employment world to perfect wife and perfect mother—without giving up much. They're hanging on by their nails (sometimes their broken nails) while trying to have it all.

On Having It All

"Women want to have it all: a successful career, a happy marriage, and loving children. What they get is work, housework, and homework." (Bruce Lansky.)

"Don't fool yourself that you are going to have it all. You are not. . . . The marvelous thing about human beings is that we are perpetually reaching for the stars. The more we have, the more we want. And for this reason, we never have it all." (Joyce Brothers.)

"Having it all doesn't necessarily mean having it all at once." (Stephanie Luetekehans.)

"When I heard there was an opening in your firm, I rushed right over."

"You can't have everything. Where would you put it?" (Steven Wright.)

When we can't have it all—when we simply can't keep our acts together—we view the flaw as being in ourselves rather than in a culture that gives us schizophrenic nonstop and high-demand messages every waking moment about what we ought to do and be.

"Not only is woman's work never done, the definition keeps changing." (Bill Copeland.)

"Isn't that supposed to be a bouquet?"

What's plaguing women is traditional cultural conditioning, operating at the unconscious level, that drives them to try to achieve far beyond what is humanly possible and indicts them when they can't do it all.

The cultural conditioning of the '50s—that tacit programming that placed men in the workplace and women in the kitchen baking cookies—served a woman's mother or grandmother well. Yet today's woman is attempting to respond to contemporary and drastically changed conditions in Western culture. If she's a homemaker, she may run a home-based business as well. If she has children, she may have an impossible list of errands to run for them and lessons to drive them to. Her sons and daughters may be playing several sports in city leagues *and* taking music or dance lessons. In addition to all this, today's woman may hold down a part-time or full-time job outside the home. She may be a single mother.

If she's old enough to remember the "good old days" when women were homemakers—*period*—she may look at those days wistfully and with considerable longing. But economic pressures are relentless, and she feels committed to helping her family succeed financially. So she does her best to cope with her multiple roles.

"Your wife can go home, but your daughter will have to stay until she completes her computer training."

"My grandmother never even owned a car, so there was never a question of holding up her end of a carpool or driving the children anywhere. Or driving herself anywhere. She didn't bowl, play tennis, golf, or go to Weight Watchers. She didn't have a standing appointment at the hairdresser's, or, saints preserve us, the nail salon." (Terry Hekker.)

Nor was this woman beset with literally dozens of messages a day, coming from all directions, telling her what she should be doing in order to be deemed an adequate woman. She knew!

"She was secure in the knowledge that, by banishing microbes, odors, and grime from the house, she was a good wife and mother." (Jean Fitzpatrick.)

Chapter 2

Changing Roles in the '90s

Seismic cultural shifts in gender roles have left women (as well as men) on shifting ground. Women's choices are immense but at the same time confounding and confusing.

"The barriers have been removed and the possibilities are great. But with these possibilities come complexity and few navigational guides." (Nicholas von Hoffman.)

On Choices

"Choices abound, and the manner in which a woman's life is divided between work and home, between her own needs and the needs of those she loves should be as individual as her fingerprints." (Ardis Whitman.)

"I had an opportunity the other day to take on more stress. I decided to go to work."

Today's choices give a woman a chance to develop herself.

*"No, I don't find it hard to maintain my femininity—
especially at forty dollars an hour."*

"When I announced I wanted to work outside the home, my husband suggested I try a little yard work. I said that wasn't exactly my definition of 'outside.'"

"Hi, Dear! What's for dinner?"

"There are some things I absolutely don't want to learn to do."

Nearly everyone faces the challenge of striking a balance between work and personal life.

"Hempstead, you've been with the firm fifteen years. Don't you think it's time to look for an apartment?"

Today's woman is a pioneer forging out unprecedented roles.

"It was after the second return to work that I realized that what we were experiencing was not simply the one-time making of a decision, but was an ongoing process that called for a continuous reevaluation. Part of this process involves learning to be at peace with the fluctuation of our needs." (Ellen Garey.)

On Releasing

Aim to release yourself from outmoded cultural programming. The trick for the woman of the '90s is to make wise choices, to be responsible in those areas that truly matter to her.

"Our biggest accomplishment may be the ability to excel and lighten up on ourselves at the same time." (Dorothy Inman.)

"'Dear, had dinner without you—
the dishes are in the sink. Love, Doris.'"

"I have a 'play the melody' philosophy. It means don't over-arrange, don't make life difficult. Just play the melody— and do it the simplest way possible." (Jackie Gleason.)

"Let's not grow old too soon and smart too late."

On Multiple Roles

Even today's homemakers are pioneers in that their internal models of "mother" may differ from the way they are living.

"If you want to worship the ground I walk on,
you had better start waxing the floors!"

"The more roles women have, the better off they are, the less likely they are to be depressed or discouraged about their lives. When we have a lot to do, we complain that it's driving us crazy—but, in fact, it's what keeps us sane." (Virginia O'Leary.)

"A woman [often] attempts to perform *perfectly* . . . [her] multiple and conflicting roles." (Marjorie Hansen Shaevitz.)

"Barbara, forget the Patterson account—bring me some Pampers!"

"Maternity leave? Oh, no, Mr. Dithers, I won't need any; I'll just have the baby on my coffee break, while I'm making oat-bran cookies for my son's third-grade bake sale and learning how to give my husband a nice shiatsu massage." (Lynn Langway.)

"Change is inevitable—except from a vending machine." (Robert C. Gallagher.)

"My needs have changed. Do you do ironing?"

Woman to optometrist: "No, I *can* see recipes. I'm just having trouble reading the stock-market reports."

"It's you!"

On the Changing Roles of Women

In the past, the man brought home the bacon. But now, "because the bacon has become so expensive, it often takes two paychecks just to afford meat on the table." (Erica Abeel.)

"Why don't you make some of the hunters women?"

"Remember, Ginger Rogers did everything Fred Astaire did—backwards and in high heels."

"What will the salary be? What will the hours be?
My chances of advancement? How about a benefits package?"

"There's no doubt about it. Women are here to say." (Earl Wilson.)

"Feel free to speak up, Hornbee—just as though you were a woman!"

"Isn't it bad enough that you'll probably outlive me?
Do you have to outearn me, too?"

"I am not hiding behind a skirt!"

"If it hadn't been for the women's movement, I couldn't have been an Avon man."

"With all these changes, what do we say to women— 'You're looking very equal today'?" (Bill Vaughn.)

"My wife and I are equals. When it snows I let *her* do the shoveling."

"One thing in which the sexes are equal is in thinking that they're not." (Franklin P. Jones.)

"How come you only believe in equal rights when it's time to pay the bills?"

On Being Single

If you're currently single, you may be tired of hearing others (many of them married people!) telling you to savor your singleness and enjoy your freedom. One author, a single man, points out that being single and lonely is a condition shared by many. But although "you may prefer to be with others . . . being alone can overcome you only if you let it." (Stephen M. Johnson.)

One single adult reports insights she gained while walking alone on the beach: "At that moment I felt particularly strong, and I was proud of myself. . . . I guess the loneliness panic that I had experienced before then became what you call lonesomeness. I would have preferred that things were different right then, but I realized I could live with the fact that they weren't." (Quoted by Stephen M. Johnson.)

"I like being single. I'm always there when I need me."

"Being single means a woman is capable of taking care of herself and coping on her own." ("Self Survey.")

COMPUTER DATING SERVICE

"No, thanks. I'm just here to reprogram the computer."

Think of being single as a time of unparalleled self-exploration.

"What if you viewed single life as an exciting challenge in which much could be learned rather than as a temporary discomfort to be endured? What could you do then?" (Stephen M. Johnson.)

"You don't trust me, do you?"

If you've just come out of a marriage, you may feel you're a severed half. Work to become a complete, whole person.

"I know you expect something in return for the movie, the flowers, and the dinner. Wait here and I'll get you a receipt."

The first year or so after becoming "suddenly single" is potentially a period of rapid growth. Treat it as a challenge.

Aim for as much personal growth as you possibly can in your singleness; take it as a challenge to do and be what you want.

"Remember, there are significant advantages to being single:

- You can talk to yourself as much as you want.
- Your cat or your dog can sleep in bed with you. . . .
- You can bring home Sara Lee cake for two and eat both portions." (Allia Zobel.)

Some characteristics of a relatively content single person include:

- realizing you're responsible for your own happiness
- treating yourself as well as any other person you love dearly
- finding, keeping, loving, and giving to friends
- becoming the classiest, most content person you know for your own sake
- investing in the welfare of others
- learning to turn loneliness to "aloneness" and, in your solitude, to embrace the joy of your own company
- making interesting things happen instead of waiting for them
- judging yourself not on the basis of who you're with but on who you are
- living in your todays instead of playing "I'll be happy when . . . "

"Right now, Roger, I need me in my life more than I need you."

On Being a Single Parent

Almost one family in four is headed by a woman.

"In many ways, single-parent households are like pioneers, exploring new frontiers in family life." (Marianne Walters and Nonny Wajchrzyk.)

*"This is the part of the evening where we learn
if you can handle rejection."*

"Well, maybe it's okay not to be normal anymore."

*"I think you should know. My mom and I
are single and we both like it that way!"*

The single mother and her kids are economically vulnerable.

"While the no-fault divorce was intended to make for a more civilized parting of ways and to affirm women's competence, what it really did was make alimony obsolete and dangerously scale down property settlements, leaving a lot of single mothers in serious trouble." (Sheila Weller.)

As a result, the single mother often gives up—willingly— many luxuries she might otherwise enjoy.

"My mother isn't like other moms. She doesn't get her nails done or soak in the tub."

The single mother assumes the equivalent of three jobs— that of absent father, of mother, and of worker.

"You made your big mistake when you called me a judgette!"

"When you're single, you have to take care of those 'other' things—the sprinkler system, the insurance adjuster, the roof that needs repair."

There isn't any way that a single mother can stretch far enough to be all things to all people, all the time.

"It doesn't take a rocket scientist to figure out why we are called 'single mothers' and our ex-husbands are called 'bachelors'!"

"The showroom was swarming with out-of-town buyers and the school nurse was telling me she could wait with Devon another ten minutes at the hospital emergency room until I arrived. When she heard my moan and all the people in the background asking me questions, she said sweetly, 'Perhaps we could have Mr. McDermott come down?' 'I'm "Mr." McDermott,' [I] wailed." (Quoted by Sheila Weller.)

"A father is not something you can buy at Woolworths." (Sheila Weller.)

As the "Adult in Charge of Everything" in the home, the single mother has a particularly difficult time balancing the home and the work front.

"My four-year-old daughter called work [when I was in the middle of an important meeting] and said that she had to speak with me. 'Mommy,' she said, 'my goldfish died. . . .'

"'Honey,' I began . . . , 'I know this is a hard time for you, but I'm very busy right now. As soon as I get home we'll have a long talk about it. Okay?'

"'But, Mommy,' she pleaded, 'I have to ask you a question *now*.'

"The meeting could wait! My child needed me. 'Go ahead, dear. Ask your question.'

"'Mommy, would it be all right if we eat him for supper?'" (Betty L. Hagerty.)

"I need these production costs . . . *Melissa, believe me, you need a training bra* . . . get me the Webster file . . . *Melissa, baby, I think* . . ."

"I'm a TV anchorwoman and this is a graphic description of what happens at work: One of my male colleagues will be talking to some researcher about fusion and I'm on the phone, going, 'Hi, Samantha, what did you do today at preschool?'"

Single mothers probably experience more guilt than any other women.

"I don't feel like I'm giving 100 percent to my family or my work."

The single woman gets "caught" in trying to do it all.

"I'm not willing to give up any of my life. Being a single parent, I overcompensate. I have to do everything. Remember the commercial, 'I can bring home the bacon, fry it up in a pan, and then never let you forget you are a man. Because I'm a *woman*!'? That's me!"

*"I'm not only a single mother, I'm also a single income, a single
plumber, a single roofer, a single gardener, a single chauffeur,
a single painter, a single carpenter, a single . . . "*

"You have to do everything, because you want everyone
to come to your house and say, 'HOW DO YOU DO IT?' 'She's
a single mother, she has a career, she keeps her house clean!'"

"The fellow that I'm dating is also a single parent who is
now raising three children. It's made our relationship easier.

"He used to say, 'Let's get together, I want to come up,' and
I would say, 'Gosh, hon, that would be great.' But inside I am
thinking—'I have to do the laundry, I've got to do the floor.
I've got to pay my bills. I have to balance the checkbook . . .'

"But now that his children are living with him, it's easier.
He says to me, 'I've got laundry to do before I come over.'"

The single mother worries about her children—"Am I doing enough?"

One single mom reports: "We live in an old mobile home. . . . When one of my son's friends, who lives in a beautiful house, ran away for a few days, I was puzzled. 'Why did he do it?' I asked. 'He has everything he could possibly wish for.'

"'Well, Mom, it's like this,' my son said matter-of-factly. 'Jimmy has a lot of environment, but not much love, and I have a lot of love but not much environment.'" (Carol Leinen.)

"It's love that makes the world go around."

"Look at it this way, Mom. It can't be any more difficult being a single child than it is being a single parent."

"Well, Mom, it's Saturday night. Do you want to get dressed up and go out for ice cream? Rent some Disney flicks? Or just hang out doing girl talk?"

The single mother can help her children learn some valuable skills.

"My kids can do their own laundry and shop the coupons just as well as I can."

Of all women, the single mother needs most to relax household standards.

"As long as I can't see it, I don't worry about it."

If you're a single mother, pat yourself on the back for what you *are* accomplishing and remember the words of two mothers to their divorced daughters:

Dear Lisa,

Sometimes moms have to work to support their children—you do it because you love them. It's not a "crime" to leave Brianne so that you can earn money to take care of her. It shows that you are responsible and that you do love her. So "chin up" and do what you have to do.

Lots of love,
Mom

"Linda, before you go to bed, say, 'Good for me! I survived another day,' because surviving in your situation is incredible." (Linda's mom.)

" . . . and God bless Mommy, and God bless Mommy's job,
and God bless Mommy's job with overtime! *"*

Single mothers, in particular, can benefit from realizing that they can't live an ordered life—especially with kids—in an unordered world.

"Nothing's wrong with survival mothering—provided everyone survives. It's impossible to be a classy mother all the time." (Vanessa L. Ochs.)

On Being a Homemaker

"Here's a quiz: What do we call the woman who does no child care but who cleans the house? A cleaning woman. What do we call the person who straightens the house and 'supervises' the children? A housekeeper. And what do we call the woman who does child care but no housework? A nanny.

"What do we call the one who does it all? A nonworking mother." (Betsy Kilday Crosby.)

And what do "nonworking" mothers do?

"They thaw hamburger in the dry cycle of the dishwasher. Walk the dog, play cards with a sick child who cheats, dress naked dolls, take phone messages for people with a social life, make Christmas ornaments out of lint. Nurse a dead fern that cost $20." (Erma Bombeck.)

When given a choice, many women choose to be homemakers and to be with their children full-time.

"Raising children—and only raising children—is a legitimate [alternative]." (Elizabeth Berg.)

Our decisions don't "have to be made once for a lifetime—and that's what's different in choices now from those of a generation ago. We assumed that each choice was forever." (Lois Wyse.)

"Every research study has confirmed that the mother has to be happy. Children thrive best when the mother feels right about what she's doing—whether she's staying at home or working outside the home." (Dana Friedman, as quoted by Josie A. Oppenheim.)

"Right now I'm balancing the checkbook—
call me back with the recipe when I'm in the kitchen."

"For two years I looked for a housekeeper. Someone warm, wonderful, motherly, loving. Then one day I realized the person I was trying to hire was me." (Linda Burton, as quoted by Marguerite Michaels.)

On Being a Wife

In the '90s women have often added eight or nine hours to their day as they've gone out into the work force for a "second shift" and haven't given up much. As a result, most women are fatigued most of the time.

"What are we doing this weekend? What's a weekend?"

What is the effect of this second shift on women? They spend fifteen fewer hours of leisure than their husbands per week, and in a year they work an extra month of twenty-four-hour days, according to one study on dual-career couples.

"Many women I could not tear away from the topic of sleep. They . . . talked about sleep the way a hungry person talks about food." (Arlie Hochschild.)

Despite these role shifts, women still tend to take care of men's needs more than the reverse.

"Here, let me butter that cob of corn for you."

"Women traditionally have been very available to their husbands for emotional support, encouragement, and help. Without even thinking about it, they provide an ear, an arm—whatever is required for as long as it is required." (Marjorie Hansen Shaevitz.)

A woman often feels pressure to take care of a man.

"When people look at a husband and see ring-around-the-collar, they don't say, 'What's the matter with him?' They say, 'What's wrong with her? Why doesn't she dress this man?'"

"My husband was an extension of me. If he didn't wear his shirttail tucked in or he didn't cut his hair on time, then I was at fault because he's my representative to the world."

A wife may become a "too-good" wife:

"While a good wife does nice things for her husband because she wants to, the too-good wife feels she has to. Focusing on his physical and emotional needs, she becomes a mother to her mate." (Dianne Hales.)

"The more competent I became, the more incompetent he became."

"OK, OK, I'm coming!"

"The too-good wife is always doing *something* because she thinks everything is either her responsibility or her fault." (Dianne Hales.)

Essentially, a woman often overfunctions for a relationship.

"My husband would get up, shower, eat his breakfast, and go off to work at 7:30. I did everything else to get everyone ready for the day and to get where they needed to go."

Overfunctioning makes a woman mad. She carries around a chronic low burn toward this man for whom she's doing too much.

"I give more than I'm getting. Let's be fair about this, please."

"Are you looking for a fight?"

"We're out of cups."

"I can forgive and forget; I just don't want my husband to forget I forgave."

One challenge is to offer the quality of mercy to men. Caught between worlds, men are feeling overwhelmed.

"Do you think you could throw me a life preserver?"

"Well, it's about time—the dawn of mankind!"

Men are being asked (while many of the old rules still apply) to adapt to a world quite different from the one they grew up in. As one man said, "I have gone where no man has gone before—I have changed a diaper."

"If you want that promotion, Mr. Hodges, you'll have to work for it. Batting your eyelashes and sighing isn't going to cut it around here."

"Only two kinds of men don't understand women— husbands and single men." (Franklin P. Jones.)

"Of course you're beginning to understand your wife—
you want another estrogen on the rocks?"

Women's gains have often been men's losses.

"My wife schedules hugs for Fridays at 9:30—kisses at 10:00!"

"Of course I love you. Now back to Dan Rather. Dan?"

"She loves me . . . she loves her job . . . she loves me . . .
she loves her job . . . she . . . "

Another challenge is for women to allow men to do more for themselves without women feeling guilty.

Confucius updated: "Husband who gets breakfast in bed is in hospital." (Alex Thein.)

"Do you have any 'Get back to work' cards for a sick husband?"

"My advice to women? Don't mother anything in whiskers." (Ruth Bryan Hudson.)

"It's your *mess!"*

"My husband does do his share, but he doesn't 'rent out.'"

On Being a Mother

Combine the roles of cook, waitress, nurse, teacher, maid, chauffeur, psychologist, psychiatrist, doctor, and banker, and what do you get? A mother.

"Working mother: What a woman becomes the instant she leaves the delivery room." (Jane S. McKay.)

"Working mother, huh?"

"The phrase 'working mother' is redundant." (Barbara Gordon.)

"I was in control of the experience of motherhood for about the first three hours of labor and since then it has become a progressively out-of-control experience for me." (Kim Wright Wiley.)

"A woman who can cope with the terrible twos can cope with anything." (Judith Clabes.)

You know you're a mother when "you can't recall where you left your glasses, but you can remember every verse of 'The Itsy-Bitsy Spider.'" (Candy Schulman.)

"What would I do without being a mother? I mean, how

else would I get burned bacon, eggshells on the floor, and six newborn kittens?" (Shirley Leuth.)

"This is my husband, my children, my dog, and my stack of unpaid bills."

"If mothers could have all their wishes, the family cat would have kittens and every neighbor would be begging to own one." (Mary Jane Thompson.)

"September is the month when millions of mothers cause thousands of school boards unnecessary expense. Did you ever try washing lipstick off a school bus?"

"A mother is neither cocky nor proud, because she knows the school principal may call at any minute to report that her child has just driven a motorcycle through the gymnasium." (Mary Kay Blakely.)

"Any mother could perform the jobs of several air traffic controllers with ease." (Usa Adther.)

"Only in America does a mother drive her kids three blocks to a physical fitness class."

"A mother is a transportation expert who has to know how to get four kids to six places in thirteen minutes." (Bill Adler.)

"It goes without saying that you should never have more children than you have car windows." (Erma Bombeck.)

"The real menace in dealing with a five-year-old is that in no time at all you begin to sound like a five-year-old." (Jean Kerr.)

"You have a wonderful child. Then, when he's thirteen, gremlins carry him away and leave in his place a stranger who gives you not a moment's peace." (Jill Eikenberry.)

"Kids are unpredictable. You never know how far up the wall they'll drive you."

*"I didn't know we knew how, but Mom says
we taught her how to climb walls."*

"Children evoke the 'jerk' response—they push and push until you turn into a jerk."

"Teenagers were put on earth to keep adults from wasting time on the telephone."

"The best way to keep teens from driving is to let the air out of the tires."

*"OK, Mom! I'll bring some friends home—
if you promise to dress like a yuppie."*

"My only advice is to stay aware, keep listening, and yell for help if you need it." (Judy Blume.)

"Motherhood is definitely not for wimps."

"And how was your day, Dear?"

On Future Women's Roles

"Women's salaries will go up. Women get paid about 70 percent of what men get; by [the year] 2000 [women] will get within 90 percent [of what men get]." (Tim Appelo.)

"No, twenty years of experience and an MBA tell me, 'This is what we will do!' . . . My woman's intuition tells me you're nuts!"

"Women entrepreneurs will start 60 percent of all new businesses." (Carol Farmer, as quoted by Tim Appelo.)

"Remember, people are known by the company they own."

"Women will have new economic power because companies will have to compete to get women. Nearly 70 percent of new jobs will be filled by women and minorities." (Betty Friedan, as quoted by Mary Ellen Schoonmaker.)

"Ten salads."

Other good news: "The successful women of the nineties are going to know how to use the opportunities that have come to their sex after 2,000 rather rough years." (Nicholas von Hoffman.)

Chapter 3

The Caretaker

In the '50s, a woman had a specific job description and a limited number of people to take care of. She could drift off to sleep knowing that she had finished her job for that day.

But in the '90s, the woman suffers from runaway caretaking. As her world and her choices have expanded, so have the number of people in it. Still, she tries to stretch far enough to care for all those around her.

"If I don't do it, who will?"

"I feel personally responsible for every grade on my children's report cards."

"Whenever my husband puts on weight I buy him underwear two sizes too small—and he always loses at least ten pounds."

"Women designate themselves 'General Managers of the Universe.'" (Gladys Allen.)

"I only took charge of all the people in the United States."

*"In other news . . . a Mrs. Roberta Smidly, mother of six,
stopped the president of the United States while he was
jogging and made him put on some long pants!"*

"I like to sit up here so I can keep an eye on all of you at one time."

"I dreamt I died and went to heaven with a bundle of good deeds tucked away in my lifetime. 'Not to worry,' I thought. 'This will be a cinch' . . . until I found myself behind Mother Teresa and heard God tell her, 'Tch, tch, tch . . . that's all you did?'"

"Not me. I'm worried about my place in heaven because with all the overtime I've put in, I'm thinking I might be overqualified!"

The caretaker always worries that she isn't doing enough.

On Caring

By virtue of her inherent giving nature, the caretaker wants to soothe pain and make others happy, but she can't stretch to meet all the needs of all.

"As women, we are often so generous, especially with ourselves, that we give little pieces of ourselves away, to almost anyone who asks." (Anne Wilson Schaef.)

*"If God didn't want me to be responsible for my children,
I would have been born a man."*

"A friend of mine keeps track of what she spends for grain to feed the birds and sends an equal amount to CARE. 'It's not fair to feed the birds,' she says, 'if you don't feed people.'" (Alice Berry.)

"If we could all hear one another's prayers, God might be relieved of some of his burden." (Ashleigh Brilliant.)

"Extending your hand is extending yourself."

"If only all the hands that reach could touch." (Mary A. Loberg.)

"My hands cannot serve all the needs to which my heart responds." (Anne Morrow Lindbergh.)

On Being Taken Care Of

The caretaker sometimes just wishes that someone else would take care of her. After all, she's taking care of others so skillfully. It would be fair.

"I know that life's not fair, but how come it's never fair in my direction?"

"If motherhood is just like any other job, why can't I call in sick?"

The caretaker has "pipe dreams":

"Daughter: 'Go sit down, Mom. I'll clean up the kitchen.'

"Police officer: 'You were only going 40? I bet our radar's on the blink again.'

"Mother-in-law: 'You certainly are a wonderful cook and housekeeper, dear.'

"Mechanic: 'It's nothing, really. I'll just tighten up the fan belt.'

"Husband: 'Tuna Surprise again? Terrific!'

"Two-year-old: 'Yes! Yes! Yes!'" (Isabel L. Livingstone.)

In waiting for people to take care of her and give her the feedback she deserves, the caretaker may suffer disappointments.

"The best I can hope for when I come home from the beautician's with a new hairstyle is that he doesn't ask me how much it cost."

"Where I work, the closest thing to a professional standing ovation sounds like, 'Thanks for doing the wash, Mom. Did you lose my other red tube sock again?' Or, 'Hey, dinner last night was great. Why'd ya make this green junk tonight?'" (Pamela Hobbs Hoffecker.)

*"After an hour of aerobics, the least you could say is
I'm looking good—not 'You're dripping wet!'"*

Sometimes the caretaker waits and waits for positive
feedback, but it is sporadic at best.

"Bless my husband, Andy, who often mumbles before
falling asleep, 'Honey, you do terrific work. I wouldn't want
your job for a million dollars.'" (Pamela Hobbs Hoffecker.)

"Charm is the quality in others that makes us more satisfied with ourselves." (Henrie Frederic.)

"Praise is something a person tells you about yourself
that you suspected all along."

"Anything scarce is valuable—praise, for example."

"Wonder is involuntary praise." (Edward Young.)

"Woman does not live by bread alone. She needs butter-
ing up once in a while."

"Just once I'd like to hear the words 'stupendous,' 'out-
rageous,' or 'magnificent,' but I'd settle for a 'super.'"

"The squeaking wheel doesn't always get the grease.
Sometimes it gets replaced." (Vic Gold.)

Since you can't count on others for emotional supplies,
it's vital not to wait for someone to create the circumstances
that make you feel good.

*"I know I'm in the wrong room. My husband is in 202 and doesn't
appreciate a caring visitor—maybe this guy does."*

Then you can simply be surprised and pleased if someone donates to your effort.

"I told my husband I was sick and he said, 'Well, don't
you worry about the dishes. You can do them tomorrow.'"

On Veteran Caretakers

A veteran caretaker is a woman who has done battle
many times in the service of trying to "fix" other people and
knows how hard it is.

"I swear you're spoiling our son, Mona."

Unfortunately, the more she knows, the less her children listen to her.

"Mother, I came to you for advice, not campfire songs."

"Kids would be more eager to accept good advice if it did not continually interfere with their plans."

The veteran caretaker is happy when her daughter gets married—now she will have grandchildren.

She won't have to retire, and she can now apply all that wisdom she learned too late to use with her own children.

"This is all I'm going to get? A grandpuppy?"

Having grandchildren gives a caretaker more people to keep track of and suffer over.

"Grandchildren are the reward for not killing your children."

"Yes, dear, I do remember how you used to drive me crazy with squirt guns."

"A grandmother will rush you to the hospital if you scratch your finger. They are seriously disturbed about germs." (Eddie, as quoted by Lee Parr McGrath.)

"A grandmother is someone who tells you the bad things

your mother did when she was a little girl." (Louise, as quoted by Lee Parr McGrath.)

"A grandmother is made to spoil you and save you from your parents." (Andy, as quoted by Lee Parr McGrath.)

"Elephants and grandchildren never forget." (Andy Rooney.)

"At bedtime, the children waited story-eyed for Grandmother." (Margaret Miller.)

"Grandma wants me to put on an apron. What's an apron?"

Sometimes veteran caretakers care for three levels of people:

"If you're a great-grandmother you can play with your great-grandchildren and not worry about getting them ready for school or seeing that they've done their homework." (Virginia Martino.)

And sometimes they do reruns with divorced children, helping them to get situated and to tidy up their lives.

*"Hi, I'm Mrs. Birnbaum, Evelyn's mother.
I'm here for your pre-date briefing."*

"If you think raising a teen is bad, just try having a child who's forty-two."

"He'll be right there—I told him to come home and put on a sweater."

"In case a nice boy looking for a home-cooked meal comes in."

"Grandchildren don't mind your wrinkles, and they don't advise you what to do." (Virginia Martino.)

But some other people do. One woman says, "I used to be the mother of four children. Now I'm the child of four mothers."

"You're seventy-two, Mother. You're too old to be gallivanting around all over the place."

"Wake me up, Mom, when you come in, because you know I can't sleep a wink until you're home."

"If you don't start coming home at an earlier hour, Mom, I'm going to ground you."

"I know what you think I ought to do—but have another think!"

"I'm too old to have to listen to anyone's advice."

"Dear Miss Know-it-all,

"I am in a dither because my daughter is running my life. What shall I do?"

"Get the heck out of that dither!"

"Mother! It's come to this?"

"When you speak to others for their own good, it's advice. When they speak to you for your own good, it's interference."

"The best advice yet given is that you don't have to take it."

On Independence of Others

"Independent: How we want our children to be as long as they do everything we say." (Joyce Armor.)

The caretaker's Achilles' heel is that she tends to consider herself indispensable, believing she can take care of others better than they can take care of themselves.

"'How can I go anywhere?' she asks bitterly. 'Without me, the kids would eat Froot Loops for dinner and the laundry hamper would burst before anyone thought to empty it.'" (Ellen Sue Stern.)

"I believe in giving George a good pep talk every morning."

"The other day my husband mentioned that he'd broken the shoelaces on his running shoes. I immediately started trying to find time to buy him new ones. He never expected me to do it. I just assumed it was my job." (Doris Helmering, as quoted by Dianne Hales.)

The caretaker tends to do too much for too many people. She's trained them to expect the services she gives (and then she complains that people want too much from her).

"'M' is for 'mom,' not 'maid.'"

"Excuse me, but I have nothing to worry about today.
Would you like to share your troubles with me?"

"The trouble with making intelligent suggestions is that you're apt to be appointed to carry them out." (Gene Brown.)

In her preoccupation to care for others, the caretaker often does so at the expense of having a clear self.

"We put our energy into taking responsibility for other people's feelings, thoughts, and behavior and hand over to others responsibility for our own." (Harriet Lerner.)

"I think you wear too much makeup, and that blouse is definitely too tight!"

When women overkill on their caretaking, others may feel resentful.

"When you do something for someone else's own good, you can bet they're not going to enjoy it."

"Have a nice day, dear, and don't come home until you do!"

"We ought to be careful not to do for a fellow what we only intended to help him do."

"One way we can do more for others is to do less."

"Often we expend great sums of time, energy, and emotion on other people's account, and expect to be appreciated for it, regardless of whether they wanted all that attention." (Ellen Sue Stern.)

The caretaker's job is to assume responsibility for her own self and to let other people do the same. Otherwise, she inhibits their independence and her own.

"We feel guilty when things go wrong. But we have to realize that it's the nature of human beings to do both wrong and right and to struggle their way to a kind of creative existence." (Carol Orsborn.)

"We cannot make people over. Our business is to make ourselves better and others happy, and that is enough to keep us busy." (Joseph Fort Newton.)

"I told him, if he's going to pot, don't do it in the house!"

"By taking responsibility for others' happiness, we invite them to become dependent—a violation that the truly healthy human spirit always vigorously refuses." (Sue Patton Thoele.)

"And then my kids said to me, 'Mom, you were right all along—we will always come to you for advice' . . . and that's when I woke up."

"I used to always buy self-improvement books, not to improve myself but to improve other people."

"When we point our finger at someone else, three fingers point back at us."

"You're spoiling that bird, Joseph!"

"If there is anything we wish to change in [others], we should first examine it and see whether it is not something that could be better changed in ourselves." (C. G. Jung.)

"This is for the kids, right?"

It was a great relief when I realized I didn't have to fix the world—just myself.

On Taking Charge

A caretaker is sometimes mad at husbands and kids or other people who are asking for a piece of her.

She thinks, "If they would just help (or help more) then my life would be under control."

"I need to take an emotional breath, step back, and remind myself who's actually in charge of my life." (Judith M. Knowlton, as quoted by Anne Wilson Schaef.)

The caretaker's primary obligation to herself is to establish boundaries.

"I am my own guardian and taskmaster."

The caretaker has limited time, energy, and resources, and there is only so much of her to give to others.

If you take care of yourself, there will be enough of you to give to them.

On Establishing Boundaries

In responding to so many people, many women suffer from privacy deprivation.

"What exactly is privacy deprivation? It's the opposite of being lonely. It's when you sneak off with a sandwich and a magazine, and you hear, 'Mom, I'm hungry.'

"It's [also] when you come home exhausted after a tyrannizing day at work and your partner demands some attention, or a friend or relative calls with a problem. It's being overstimulated by people, noise, and everyday problems— and not finding a moment or place to concentrate, refresh yourself, or experience some enjoyment *all by yourself.*" (Ilene Springer.)

"The human animal needs a freedom seldom mentioned: freedom from intrusion. He needs a little privacy quite as much as he wants understanding or vitamins or exercise or praise." (Phyllis McGinley.)

"The problem is that we've begun to think of privacy as an expendable luxury, not as a need." (Harriet B. Braiker.)

Carving out a private place for ourselves is difficult; a woman feels guilty if she isn't taking care of others or if she is taking care of herself.

"One day as I was cleaning house, my three-year-old son

asked, 'Mom, do you want me to clean while you play?'"
(Jean Gillies.)

"That's OK, dear, I'll pick up your dirty socks."

To establish boundaries, a caretaker has to protect her
time. In the '90s, time, like money, has to be budgeted.

"We have a choice. Do we spend fifteen minutes on the
phone with someone who wants to sell us carpet shampoo
and try to get out of hurting anyone's feelings, or do we
spend that time on ourselves?"

In essence, a woman defaults on *herself* unless she takes
periodic breaks from meeting the needs of others.

"The best way for a woman to have a few minutes to
herself is to start doing the dishes." (Arthur Godfrey.)

"I have toyed with the idea of hiring a baby-sitter just so
I could take a bath." (Rachel Pollack.)

"A [caretaker] need only step into the shower to be
instantly reassured she is indispensable to every member of
her family." (Lynn M. Williams.)

"I need to be alone for a while, so I've decided to hike through the woods by the lake—but I will be in beeper range."

"I find myself giving strict instructions to my family that I don't want to be disturbed, and then five minutes later I'm checking with them to see if anyone wants me for anything."

"I've written down everything you need to know about being on your own. Here's my toll-free beeper number, your emergency medical card, and a network of mothers across the country who will get back to me if you have any problems . . ."

"How do I get my children's attention? There's nothing to it. I just sit down and look comfortable." (Allein Klein.)

Every woman needs to create her own "prime time" by being on her list of things to do every day.

"If you are always last on your list of priorities and your number never comes up, the cards are stacked against you." (Sanford Matthews, M.D., and Maryann Bucknum Brinley.)

"This is called 'The Long Weekend.' It smells so bad that no one will come near you for three days, so then you can relax and rest."

"You get me twenty-three hours a day, but this hour is mine."

"Sorry. I'm off-duty right now."

"I cannot come because this is my hour to be alone." (Anne Morrow Lindbergh.)

And every woman needs to take longer stretches of time to refurbish herself.

*"Do you want to get away from it all,
or do you want 'all' to go with you?"*

"If anyone needs anything while I'm gone, just call 'Dial-a-Prayer.'"

*"Your wife has put herself on layaway, sir.
You can redeem her around Christmas."*

"Hello, Dial-a-Prayer?"

The caretaker also needs to reserve some money to refurbish herself.

"Who handles the money in your family?"

"When there's enough money, I'll take care of myself."

It's vital that you put yourself on the same plane as those other people for whom you care so diligently. It's time for you to invest in yourself.

"I don't want something that just says 'money.'
I want something that says 'megabucks'!"

"I'm going to invest in me, too. I'm worth it."

On Saying No

"I find it hard to say no. I worry that if I do, they'll wonder, 'What on earth does she *do* all day?'"

*"I love to go grocery shopping with my mom—
she has no junk food resistance."*

For a caretaker, saying no is a value-laden issue. She doesn't want to reject anyone or to be rejected. Therefore, her self-esteem is on the line every time she considers saying yes or no.

"Women who need outside validation have trouble saying no."

Women who say no comfortably "feel entitled to have a life of their own. Entitled to decide what really matters to them. Entitled to set their own priorities. Entitled to make their own choices." (Judith Viorst.)

"'Available on demand' is no longer one of my mottoes."
"I say no when other people can do it for themselves."

*"Let me follow this logic, Son. You're 38 years old, you rip
your pants, and you expect me to mend them?"*

Saying no should have to do with your priorities, interests, and available time, not your very value as a human
being. When saying no, you don't have to give a reason.

"I regret that I cannot comply with your request. So that
you may know that my refusal is final, I give no reason."
(Dean Acheson.)

"When I find myself hedging or hesitating, I take that to
mean that I'm feeling overwhelmed about saying yes. A
delayed response gives me time to decide how a yes
response relates to my priorities."

If you don't set limits, you dissipate your energies and neglect the people and activities that are truly important to you, as this woman did:

"Ease up, Charles—I've only cut you off for two days!"

"Did you say no with an exclamation point,
question mark, or simple period?"

If you're wishy-washy, you communicate to other people that there's a chance you can be sold.

"If she says no with a twinkle in her eye, ask again—she's weakening!"

"The easiest way to get out of anything is usually through the door." (Hester Mundis.)

"One of the hardest jobs for a parent is making a child realize that 'No' can be a complete sentence." (Earl Wilson.)

"You don't have to shout."

"When I say no, I mean 'I mean it!'"

"When, against one's will, one is highly pressured into making a hurried decision, the best answer is always no, because no is more easily changed to yes than yes is changed to no." (Charles E. Nelson.)

Saying no judiciously protects others from your resentment when you say yes and don't mean it. Never say yes without being willing to release others from being responsible for your choice.

"I hate it when you rush me, Harold!"

Saying no conserves your energy for your own priorities and protects you from traps of your own making.

"Yes, she's in a good mood—so I'm not about to let you spoil it!"

Saying no is a way of saying yes to yourself.

On Women and Houses

It's a caretaker's traditional duty to keep a house in perfect working order, and she typically feels discombobulated if her house isn't in order too.

"Some friends called, and without telling me, my husband said, 'Sure, come on over!' When they came, he didn't take them into the living room. He took them downstairs where all the laundry was lying on the sofa. He just shoved the underwear over and invited them to sit down. He couldn't understand why I was so humiliated."

*"Oh, she won't be mad. . . . Honey, I brought
a few board members home for dinner."*

A woman's worth is often tied to the cleanliness of her house. In fact, a dirty house constitutes a woman's shame.

"The only thing domestic about me is that I was born in this country." (Phyllis Diller.)

"A dirty sock on the floor is a mark on my character."

"My house is so messy that I would be embarrassed if I died."

"If I'm ever in an accident, please burn my house down."

"My personal dirt and clutter threshold changes when I know my mother is coming."

"Things went pretty well the last time my mother visited. She only cleaned one thing."

"Every woman who walks through that door is a member of the Universal Mother Force." (A *Cathy* cartoon by Cathy Guisewite.)

"I remember my mother talking to me about the 'joys of dusting.'"

"Dinner will be ready as soon as Mother finishes her inspection of my housecleaning."

"Show me a home where the buffalo roam, and I'll show you a very messy house."

"Show me a woman whose home is always ready for unexpected company, and I'll show you a woman who's too tired to entertain." (Beryl Pfizer.)

"I took my husband around the house showing him everything I did today, and he got tired."

"Cleaning your house while your kids are still growing is like shoveling the walk before it stops snowing." (Phyllis Diller, as quoted by Elaine Cannon.)

"What's done is done . . . for about five minutes." (Beryl Pfizer.)

"Our house has tides like the ocean. Each morning,

debris is carted upstairs, to the front room, the bathroom or clothes hamper. Next morning another tide rolls in." (Jean Gillies.)

"Just when I get the place looking like I want it to."

"Never in recorded history has housework ever been finished."

"Don't tell me you still clean your children's place?"

"You can always tell a home with a five-year-old in it. You have to wash the soap before you use it." (Richard Celeste.)

"The trouble with having your own home is that no matter where you sit, you're looking at something you should be doing." (Franklin Folge.)

"My nervous disorder made me jump up to dust things."

"The trouble with running a house is I can't get anyone to do an honest day's work anymore—including, unfortunately, myself." (Beryl Pfizer.)

On Releasing from Houses

Today's women aren't worrying so much about their houses. They're giving up their guilt and learning to live a complex life more easily.

In the '90s "dust bunnies will proliferate at the rate of real bunnies." (Tim Appelo.)

"It's only lately that I've realized that I'm not alone. Lots of other women are beating themselves up inside every day of their lives because their houses—like mine—won't stay together."

"What do you mean, you hate this house . . . ?"

"A spotless house is the sign of a misspent life." (Ann McGee-Cooper.)

If my house is messy, it has nothing to do with my inherent worth—just my priorities, my available time, and my stress level.

"Taking care of a house is simply a job, not a quest for sainthood."

"I refuse to let dirty laundry be an emotional event in my life."

"I release my self-esteem from my house. Doing housework is only a job—not a comment on one's worth."

"A dirty house does not bespeak a dirty soul." (Elizabeth R. Crow.)

"However, housework *does* make me ugly."

"A stack of dirty dishes is not a sign of a neglected house. It's just a sign that people like to eat." (Jean Gillies.)

"A woman who doesn't like kitchen duty isn't a female failure; she is a woman who doesn't like kitchen duty." (Elaine Cannon.)

"Say, isn't that my golf cart?"

"A sign on my coffee table reads, 'Dust is a protective covering.'"

"With any luck you may grow as myopic about dust balls as your husband is." (Kathleen Fury.)

"I'm not a compulsive housekeeper; I just clean when I have a compulsion."

"Housework is not on my list of top ten."

"If my house gets too messy, I just call the troop together and everybody picks up 500 things."

"Oh, yeah, how come cleaning the house isn't a family sport?"

"If you've come to see me, come anytime; if you came to see my house, make an appointment."

"If there are no clean glasses in the dishwasher or cupboards, look in the sink. I know you'll find one there that's begging to be washed!"

"What a new idea! I had this friend who came to visit and it dawned on me . . . I didn't have to do anything." (Mary, as quoted by Anne Wilson Schaef.)

Chapter 4

The Juggler

"A thousand expectations . . . a million demands . . . every second of every day, a reeling blur of zero control." (A *Cathy* cartoon by Cathy Guisewite.)

The juggler is the production and efficiency expert who has mottoes that serve her:

"Never walk upstairs without something in your hand."

"If it weren't for the last minute, nothing would get done."

"It doesn't take *me* a whole day to do a half day's work."

"Hi, Daddy! Mom forgot something at the store."

The juggler is in perpetual motion, pushing nonstop, twenty-four hours a day, to squeeze more into her split-second schedule.

"The juggler's mind is racing to take care of details, calculating and cataloging what to do next."

"Sometimes I wish I had suction cups to hold me down." (Pam, as quoted by Anne Wilson Schaef.)

"At home I'm always computing what my next move is going to be—like swiping at a cobweb the next time I go through a room or carrying a garbage can to the other end of the house."

On the home front, the juggler loves the new cordless phone because now she can get her work done and socialize at the same time without feeling guilty. She practices dovetailing her activities:

*"Make use of your time. As you round first base, review
your math homework—between second and third,
maybe a little history—and as you slide home . . ."*

In the office the juggler doesn't take breaks and she eats
on the run. She's usually moving from one emergency to
another, and everything has to have a work purpose.

"Sitting still at work drives me crazy. If there's a lull, I
find something to do, like filing or sit-ups."

*"Gentlemen, I've always said 'time is money,'
and I practice what I preach!"*

This high-wattage woman often combines "at home work" with office work throughout her day.

"My mom is a woman of the nineties. She reads
Good Housekeeping *and* The Wall St. Journal!*"*

On Lists

Jugglers are notorious list makers. They eat, sleep, and breathe lists, and they are proud of this fact.

"That's just today's list!"

They use lists to keep the synapses in their brains from completely frying.

"Lists are great for [people] who have more details to attend to than can be stored in one brain." (Joan Lippert.)

"My first list."

The juggler is on the line every moment to perform, at the same time collecting more things to do and making never-ending lists. And lists of her lists. And color-coded lists of those lists . . .

"Mom, I need a ride to Sally's.
Could you pencil me in on today's schedule?"

"Oh, the pleasures of lists—endless, ongoing lists. Lists of things to do, places to go, people to see, . . . books to read. Shopping lists, laundry lists, Christmas-card lists. Lists scratched on the backs of old envelopes, lists scrawled on a chalkboard in the kitchen. Lists no bigger than a postage stamp stuck in a wallet. . . .

"The danger, of course, is that lists may enslave. Suddenly a small scrap of paper becomes a despot. You're so busy checking your list you don't notice life going by." (Jeanine Larmouth.)

A juggler's life, in fact, may be taken over by lists.

"In order to keep the various little boxes in working order, your days must be terribly structured and organized. You live by a list, with each moment accounted for. When something goes wrong or the unexpected occurs, it becomes nearly impossible to keep things straight." (Ellen Sue Stern.)

"I put 'Quit making so many lists' on my list of things to do."

If you're a juggler, take charge. Challenge the tyranny of your lists.

"Have you finished reading your refrigerator?"

"When I look at my list of things to do, I always draw a circle around one or two items that I absolutely am *not* going to do today."

Perpetual list making will keep you focused on failures. The trick is to start focusing on successes.

"No, I don't dress for success—I work for it!"

"I do my chore first and *then* I put it on the list and cross it off."

On Pushing

"When confronted by frustration, we often feel driven to do battle—to solve a problem quickly and at all costs. If the problem fails to yield to this initial pushing, we then assume that the answer lies in pushing that much harder." (Patricia Carrington.)

"I can get an amazing number of things done—if I don't do anything else."

"So __that's__ how she does it!"

The juggler is always pushing, ever pressing to become more efficient and to do fancier juggling tricks.

"There are only twenty-four hours in a day, but the [juggler] tries to squeeze in more. Like the airlines, she schedules appointments when she's already overbooked. Consequently she's impatient, often in the position of having to apologize, and almost always running behind." (Ellen Sue Stern.)

"Because of circumstances beyond my control, I'm on time."

"I have to jog in a sweat suit. Otherwise, no one knows I'm exercising—they just think I'm late."

"God put me on earth to accomplish a certain number of things. Right now I am so far behind, I will never die."

"I'm working so hard on my time management that I don't get anything done."

"The quickest way to do many things is to do one thing at a time."

"It's not easy taking my problems one at a time when they refuse to get in line." (Ashleigh Brilliant.)

"It's easy to put first things first, but it's awfully hard to put next things next." (Beryl Pfizer.)

"One good thing about rushing is that I'm going so fast that I'm not aware that I can't possibly do all the things I'm doing."

"When you're in too much of a rush, you're liable to pass more than you catch up with." (Barry Farber.)

"Most . . . pursue pleasure with such breathless haste that they hurry past it." (Soren Kierkegaard.)

"The feeling of being hurried is not usually the result of living a full life and having no time. It is, rather, born of a vague fear that we are wasting our life." (Eric Hoffer.)

"In making a living today, many no longer leave room for life." (Joseph R. Sizoo.)

"There is more to life than increasing its speed." (Jennifer James.)

"People sometimes forget that a rat race can be won only by a rat." (Paul Palmer.)

On Paying the Price

As a juggler, you keep yourself "so busy *doing* that you have little time to *feel*. The rush of perpetual motion creates an illusion of purpose, but in truth, you barely have time to get where you're going, much less know if it's the right place to be." (Ellen Sue Stern.)

"It's a good thing I'm living in the past—
I'd have a heck of a time handling today's problems!"

"Jugglers aren't paid very well, and sometimes they get hit on the head with balls they have in the air." (Anne Wilson Schaef.)

Sometimes the juggler schedules so tightly and commits to so much that her world comes crashing down.

"Our engines get overrevved. . . . We are hysterically trying to catch up, and things keep getting worse. The car stalls, your appointment stands you up, and you get a phone call from the school nurse telling you to pick up your child. And then your mother calls to ask you how you are doing." (Carol Orsborn.)

"Worst case of juggler burnout I've ever seen!"

At times, the juggler's production level suffers as she becomes fragmented.

"I will get started with one thing—and then before I finish, I see something else that I need to work on, so I will do that. By the end of the hour or the day, I will have ten things going and not have finished any of them. I have spread myself so thin that all I do is create chaos."

The juggler can't stop to regroup or to lead the examined life, because her worth is tied to her production.

"You are far more than the sum of what you produce." (Jennifer James.)

In her whirl of frenetic activity, the juggler often doesn't have time for the people who are most important to her and for whom she is pushing so hard. Her husband may complain, "You're too busy to sit down and just talk to me. I already have a fine mother. What I need is a wife."

"My husband wants me to sit down and talk with him. He always wonders, 'What's her hurry?'"

"It's amazing how much can be accomplished in a single day if you don't stop to have a conversation with someone who jogs to work, is going through a divorce, has quit smoking or has a new grandchild." (Don Epstein.)

Among those people she may be inadvertently neglecting may be herself.

"I went outside to relax, but I noticed the house needs painting, weeds are growing wild in my garden, the faucets leak, my roses need pruning, the . . ."

"I had forgotten what spare time felt like—so when I finally got some I blinked and it was gone."

On Stopping

"For the juggler to cease her 'busyness' means to come face-to-face with her center. The challenge is to explore it, experiment with it, make friends with it." (Carol Orsborn.)

"It's four hundred blank pages so you can just doodle!"

"The poor dear. It's the only place she can go to relax."

"I feel like something's really wrong if I'm not going full throttle."

To temper busyness, the juggler has to master the command "STOP!"

When the juggler does stop—momentarily—she tends to get mad at people (namely men) who take relaxing in stride.

"My husband will come home and sit back in the easy chair, get a soda, relax with some popcorn. Do I decide to sit down with him? No; instead I get angry. He's so relaxed—and I have a million things to do! So I jump up and do all these things—and resent him. It doesn't bother him that his stuff is all over the work room and the yard hasn't been mowed for a month!"

"You've got to learn how to relax."

Men aren't as plagued by guilt as women when they stop.

"Men, whether they're putting up storm windows or checking the quarterly sales figures, always seem to feel they're doing the right thing at the right time. Nothing whispers in their ear, 'Shouldn't you be painting the garage instead?' . . . But women feel that whatever we're doing, short of maybe saving the children from a burning building, we ought to be doing something else." (Barbara Holland.)

On Just "Being"

"Women's normal occupations in general run counter to creative life or contemplative life or saintly life." (Anne Morrow Lindbergh.)

"One should lie empty, open, choiceless, as a beach waiting for a gift from the sea." (Anne Morrow Lindbergh.)

"I'm exiting the Holland Tunnel and should be in the office in about an hour . . ."

Knowing how to stop aids the juggler in increasing the quality of life.

"The rational side of the brain that loves making lists—that keeps things organized and controlled and adores prioritizing—doesn't know beans about the quality of life." (Carol Orsborn.)

Stopping requires a juggler to become a "human being" rather than a "human doing."

"If you can spend a perfectly useless afternoon in a perfectly useless manner, you have learned how to live." (Lin Yutang.)

On Celebrating the Temporary

"Don't wait until tomorrow—live today.

"Don't wait until all the problems are solved or all the bills are paid.

"You will wait forever. Eternity will come and go and you will still be waiting." (Clyde Reid.)

"You don't get to choose how you're going to die. Or

when. You can only decide how you're going to live. Now."
(Joan Baez.)

"There is no time like the pleasant." (George E.
Bergman.)

"The day is a shoe to be walked in." (Steve Orlen.)

"Because it's just too nice a day to spend inside!"

"Normal day, let me be aware of the treasure you are."
(Mary Jean Irion.)

"Seize this day! Begin now! Each day is a new life. Seize
it. Live it. For in today already walks tomorrow." (David Guy
Powers.)

"One of the wonders of life is just that—the wonders of
life." (Bille Copeland.)

"Idleness is not doing nothing. Idleness is being free to
do anything." (Floyd Dell.)

"Don't bug Mom. She's having a ball!"

"To be idle requires a strong sense of personal identity." (Robert Louis Stevenson.)

"It's a great art to saunter." (Henry David Thoreau.)

"She walked as though she had no place to go and all day to get there." (Catherine R. Wright.)

"Yes, there is a Nirvana; it is in leading your sheep to a green pasture, and in putting your child to sleep, and in writing the last line of your poem." (Kahlil Gibran.)

*"Since I get up every morning with you, I thought it
was about time to spend some time with you."*

"We do not remember days; we remember moments."
(Cesare Pavese.)

"Seize from every moment its unique novelty, and do not
prepare your joys." (Andre Gide.)

"The best way to pay for a lovely moment is to enjoy it."
(Richard Bach.)

"For a feeling that makes you very much alive, sensitive
to every movement of your being and aware of the vibra-
tions of your environment, there's nothing like a good sun-
burn." (Paul Sweeney.)

"Sometimes I would almost rather have people take
away years of my life than take away a moment." (Pearl
Bailey.)

"Today is the first day of the rest of your life—unless you
live on the other side of the international date line, in which
case yesterday was the first day of the rest of your life."

Chapter 5

The Guilt Sponge

A guilt sponge soaks up blame for anything that goes wrong in her life.

"Why am I the only one who feels guilty when the kids need haircuts or the paper towels run out?"

"Show me a woman who doesn't feel guilty and I'll show you a man." (Erica Jong.)

"Mom, you've got to stop blaming yourself."

Guilt sponges have long, overbooked guilt festivals about nearly everything nearly all the time.

"If it's true the mind is like a sponge, I wish I could

squeeze mine out once in a while and get rid of stuff I don't need anymore." (Beryl Pfizer.)

"Guilt is the hardest emotion to deal with because it is so pervasive it is almost invisible. It's like smog." (James Purcell.)

It's a good thing that guilt doesn't smell. Otherwise, we'd all have to walk around with deodorizers. A guilt sponge feels guilty if—

- she doesn't begin her diet—today
- she throws away a soda pop can that could be recycled
- she thinks about her cellulite
- she sees her unused exercise bicycle
- her cleaning lady finds a cobweb in her shower

"Believe me, dear, the ants and aphids are not going to blame you for their homelessness."

The ultimate guilt is feeling guilty over feeling guilty. On second thought, the ultimate guilt is feeling guilty over *not* feeling guilty.

"I feel guilty telling my therapist I still feel guilty all the time—I hate to hurt her feelings."

On the Impact of Guilt

Guilt sponges are haunted by guilt if they go off duty.

"Many of us still feel guilty if we are anything less than an emotional service station to others." (Harriet Lerner.)

We "fear that we're going to disappoint someone we love, fear that they'll discover that we aren't all they want us to be, fear that they'll stop loving us. For women, no threat could be more terrifying than the loss of love." (Dianne Hales, "You've Done Your Best. Why Do You Still Feel Guilty?")

Guilt catches women coming and going:

"One woman said that when she does the dishes, she feels guilty that she isn't playing with the kids, and when she plays with the kids, she feels guilty that the dishes are sitting there." (Nancy Fasciano.)

Unfortunately, many women have a tendency to feel guilt.

"I've come to realize that whatever you do, you feel you're wrong. If you work part-time, full-time or stay at home, you're sure you should have made a different choice. Guilt comes with the territory." (Ellen Galinsky and Judy David.)

Guilt sponges usually feel guilty over things they can't control and for which they're not responsible.

"If only I'd nursed my son longer, he wouldn't be having problems in fourth-grade math."

"I should have put mine in the right kindergarten."

Most women practice "'magical thinking'—the superstitious belief that our most insignificant acts can literally work wonders." (Francine Prose.)

"Women keep a special place in their heart for sins they have never committed." (Cornelia Otis Skinner.)

Women who have children suffer pervasive "mother guilt."

"Most mothers feel murderous at one time or another in their lives and feel almost as guilty as if they had actually done the dreadful deed." (Lynn Caine.)

"It's impossible to see a child suffer even a mild indisposition, let alone a bad toothache, without feeling we have failed to protect him or her." (Suzanne Ruta.)

"I felt guilty every time I put my child down for a nap. It was like, in losing that time, he might not get a college education."

"[Women] are trained in this culture to believe they are responsible for other people's happiness, so that when anybody is unhappy, women think *automatically* that they should fix things." (Lynn Caine.)

*"It's my fault. When I was carrying her I was
frightened by a vacuum cleaner."*

Though guilt is a common emotion among women, men
also feel guilt, of course; but men usually don't experience
guilt as intensely as women do. Guilt rarely plagues a man
because he's reading the paper rather than doing the dishes,
but a woman may feel like a slouch.

"A man can take a sick child to a doctor without it even
entering his brain that he might somehow be responsible for
the illness."

"Sorry, I can't feel guilty over not feeling guilty." (A man.)

On Dealing with Guilt

There is a difference between earned and unearned guilt.

Earned guilt—"over the times we are indeed rude, irre-
sponsible or dishonest—can goad us to do and to be better.
Unearned guilt merely slows us down, gets in the way, occasionally brings us to a screeching halt. It's hard to forge
ahead with our lives when we're constantly apologizing for
stepping out of line." (Dianne Hales.)

Unearned guilt flows from the "shoulds" and "oughts" that burn in a woman's brain.

"Our shoulds are often ugly, scolding voices that choke joy. They are taskmasters who overflow with criticism and run dry on praise." (Carol van Klompenburg.)

The challenge is to examine your "shoulds" and "oughts": I should keep the house clean. I should be slim. I should be less inhibited. Then consciously choose the ones you want to embrace.

"Before we end this argument, we've got to decide who gets stuck with the guilt."

"You can 'should' all over yourself, but all you end up needing is a bigger shovel."

The objective is to achieve maturity.

"I seem to have an awful lot of people inside me." (Dame Edith Evans.)

Put names and faces on the "shoulds" and "oughts" and decide, one by one, whether you agree with the voices that tell you how to feel, think, believe.

"Well, I'm back from my assertiveness class. What's for dinner?"

And we need to aim to achieve the "mature conscience":

"The mature conscience is a guardian of what we have decided to revere. It keeps us alert to our highest visions of what is good and beautiful and true. It is the inner compass that guides us on the path we have chosen." (Sam Keen.)

Chapter 6

The Perfectionist

I want to be the kind of woman who can wear a white sweater to a power lunch without spilling soy sauce. Who has only good hair days. Who has never walked into an important presentation trailing a train of toilet paper from her shoe." (Margo Kaufman.)

The perfectionist sets impossibly high goals for herself and then endlessly berates herself because she can't achieve them.

"It isn't only a matter of 'having it all.' It is a matter of having it all be perfect." (Laura Berman.)

"You have everything planned for the year?
Good heavens, Carol, it's only January 2."

"It's a wonder there aren't more perfectionists. Society, after all, exhorts us to have perfect teeth, perfect skin; to be the perfect mother, the perfect wife; to cook the perfect meal; to enjoy the perfect evening." (Kerry McPhedran.)

"When you aim for perfection, you discover it's a moving target." (George Fisher.)

"Perfectionists simply do not know where to draw the line, when to say, 'I've done enough. This is good enough.'" (Baila Zeitz, as quoted by Kathryn Stechert.)

"Perfectionists are like Olympic athletes practicing the high jump. Instead of jumping the hurdle and saying, 'Hey, I did great,' perfectionists raise the hurdle."

"My expectations—which I extended whenever I came close to accomplishing my goals—made it impossible ever to feel satisfied with my success." (Ellen Sue Stern.)

"Women often fail to recognize the difference between doing something competently and doing something perfectly." (Janet P. Wollersheim.)

"We're rewiping clean counters. That's what we're doing."

"Instead of savoring their 'high marks,'" perfectionists "are haunted by their 'incompletes.'" (Ellen Sue Stern.)

"[Perfectionists] throw away what they could have by insisting on perfection, which they cannot have, and looking for it where they will never find it." (Kathryn Stechert.)

"There's something out of place in this room and <u>I can't find it!</u>"

"I wanted everything in my life to be perfect—except my bathroom scale."

On the Impact of Perfectionism

"If we don't do it all, we feel guilty; if we do, we wear ourselves out."

"I did everything right, but I still wasn't perfect—just tired."

The first risk a woman incurs is in trying to *be* perfect.

The second risk a woman incurs is *running into* a lurking perfectionist. Quite frankly, perfectionists are hard to take (even if you *are* one).

"There are certain things people shouldn't discuss in public, and one of them is that they've got their Christmas cards all addressed by the middle of November." (Jane Goodsell.)

"When anyone mentions [a perfectionist] to me, I imagine her with parsley in her ears." (Susan Mirow, as quoted in "Chemical Depression.")

"A perfectionist is someone who takes great pains and gives them to other people."

"See, I told you—even her dust is neat."

In fact, encountering a perfectionist can be the last straw. The perfectionist has perfect children.

"Her children are always well-matched."

"When they sit on Santa's lap, they ask for world peace." (Mary McBride.)

She organizes and controls others to keep her world intact.

"I treated my children like projects, efficiently managing and orchestrating their lives, often at the expense of their feelings." (Ellen Sue Stern.)

"I used to despise Christmas because after the kids put the ornaments on the tree and wrapped the gifts I felt compelled to rearrange the tree. Sometimes I even bribed my kids to let me redo their presents because I didn't want imperfect presents under the tree."

"My husband thinks that if I wasn't such a perfectionist, I'd be a perfect wife."

"My marriage improved when I stopped trying to be the perfect little wife and became a woman."

On Releasing from Perfectionism

"Remember, one nice thing about being imperfect is the joy it brings to others."

"You don't need my help. You're <u>perfect</u> the way you are!"

"Don't try to be such a perfect girl, darling. Do the best you can without too much anxiety or strain." (Jesse Barnard.)

"Why, yes, dear, it looks perfect. Even the rice is lined up in neat little rows."

"Release yourself from a task when the joy of doing it well gives way to fear of not doing it perfectly." (Kerry McPhedran.)

"One day not long ago—I don't remember exactly when—I clambered off the perfection treadmill. Today, I am an aspiring connoisseur of the beauty of imperfection, a believer in the virtues of not even trying for perfect. A devotee of the inexact, praiser of the imprecise, champion of the (occasional) failure." (Laura Berman.)

*"Her paté needs work, her curtains didn't match the rug,
there was no order in her cupboards—and she calls
herself a released perfectionist!"*

"There are no medals at the end of this life for having achieved everything perfectly."

*"I tried to make my company perfect. I couldn't do it, so I sold it and
made a bundle. That's when I realized 'not-so-perfect' ain't so bad!"*

"Why am I so happy? Because I have low standards."

On Tempering Perfection

"For the recovering perfectionist, 'good enough' should be the rallying cry." (Kathryn Stechert.)

"Sometimes good enough may mean 99th percentile and sometimes it may mean 20th. Good enough uses a different measure, the measure of purpose." (Carol van Klompenburg.)

I'm beginning to like the concept of a good-enough dinner or a clean-enough room. Thinking that way makes me feel like a good-enough woman. We could benefit by doing some things with "good enough" in mind.

"To you it's a perfect mess, but to me everything is in a perfectly logical place."

Don't take yourself so seriously.

"When I get in a pinch, I say to myself with firmness, 'So what?'"

Give yourself credit for what you have accomplished.

"God made our arms long enough to pat our backs and our legs too short to kick ourselves."

Think *average:*

"If I do better than average, then I'll be pleasantly surprised."

Simply cut corners and delegate.

"You can simplify any job by getting someone else to do it." (Hester Mundis.)

"No-iron clothes aren't really a new idea. I remember when my children were little, I sometimes folded the wash and sat on it." (Jean Gillies.)

"An organized person is one who is too lazy to look for things." (JoAnn Thomas.)

"I got tired of being a perfectionist. I got messy, he complained, and now he cleans the house. Am I smart or what?"

Separate your achievement from your worth: "I am who I am—not what I do." And finally, let your goals guide, not tyrannize, you.

"Ideals are stars to steer by. They are not a stick to beat ourselves with." (Barbara Smith.)

Words from Released Perfectionists

"I've given up my quest for perfection and am shooting for five good minutes in a row." (A *Cathy* cartoon by Cathy Guisewite.)

"I believe that ironing is just for women who get nervous about wrinkles."

"My husband and I eat from the three basic food groups—canned, frozen and take-out." (Mary Pledge Peterson.)

*"It's the latest fashion statement! It gives
the illusion of a home-cooked meal."*

"If Betty Crocker doesn't make it, neither do I."

"If we don't make our bed every morning, it should not be a matter calling for twenty lashes." (Doris Lund.)

"As long as I can't see it—meaning as long as I can sweep it under a rug—I'm not going to worry about it."

"If my microwave finger is too tired, I just don't heat the pizza."

"Any plant in my house has to count on having near-death experiences."

A released perfectionist, without flinching, can—

• Scotch-tape her unraveled hem

• smash store-bought brownies so they look homemade

• put her kids to bed fully dressed so they're ready for the baby-sitter in the morning

• pass a woman in a grocery store who has a perfectly organized shopping cart without even flinching

• hide dishes in the oven when company is coming

• send borderline flu cases to school

• buy her homemade bread from the neighbor

- mend a hole in her husband's pants pocket with a rubber band
- insist that her husband do his own rubber-band repair
- buy a dress just as nice as the one she could make
- make a note to pick up gummy worms for her five-year-old at the same time she's talking to the president of the company
- chop down the tree instead of canning the apples
- buy products that say "Tastes homemade"
- simply turn over the compost in her children's bedrooms once every six months

"Dr. Larsen, I enjoyed your comments. Does this mean I don't have to use the dog food cookbook my husband got me?"

Chapter 7

The Pleaser

Pleasers look outward for clues as to how they're doing. With approval, their self-esteem soars—temporarily. With disapproval, they feel "nothingized"—reduced to a zero.

"If someone says I've done well, the stock in myself goes up ten thousand points. If they say I've done poorly, I lose everything—all in one shot."

"I always thought I was nothing unless I was valued by a significant other person who would give my life more meaning."

"We forfeit three-fourths of ourselves in order to be like other people." (Schopenhauer.)

"However much we guard ourselves against it, we tend to shape ourselves in the image others have of us. It is not so much the example of others we imitate, as the reflection of ourselves in their eyes and the echo of ourselves in their words." (Eric Hoffer.)

"I don't know what the recipe for success is, but I know that the recipe for failure is trying to please everyone."

A pleaser tends to assume the impossible task of keeping everyone else happy, often at her own expense.

She *hates* disapproval.

"Two of my neighbors told me they didn't feel like I was paying the baby-sitter enough money. I was crushed for three days."

"You're allergic to life."

She personalizes events in her life:

"My next-door neighbor put up a 'For Sale' sign on her house and I wondered if I had done something wrong. I wanted to put up a sign in front of my own house that said: 'Was it something I said?'"

"When I said, 'I don't know how you keep up with your heavy schedule,' I did __not__ imply you were fat!"

She makes elaborate excuses:

"Sally Forth: I would have been in earlier to work but just as we were ready to leave Hillary told me she had a birthday party after school today. We had to stop at a gas station to get a present because nothing else was open. Then all they had for wrap was a brown bag, so we had to buy some markers and draw designs on it.

"Fellow office worker: I love your excuses. Everyone else just oversleeps." (A *Sally Forth* cartoon by Greg Howard.)

She over-apologizes:

"I'm sorry to drive you crazy."

And she discounts her own perceptions and opinions:

"I don't see it your way so I must be wrong."

"You're a sucker for anyone who wants to make a quick buck!"

She worries about how she's doing:

"Am I fitting in here?"

"Will they invite me back?"

"Did I say the wrong thing?"

"Do they like me?"

"Am I wearing the right dress?"

"She never thinks, 'What do I want to say?' She thinks, 'What does he want to hear?' She never asks someone else, 'What do you have in mind?' Instead she rushes to supply what she imagines the other person desires." (Natalie Shainess.)

She feels undeserving:

"My last promotion? I just got lucky."

"Anyone can be a winner if they work as hard as I do."

And she avoids declaring herself:

"I can't come to dinner because I'm on a diet that is so embarrassing I can't possibly eat in front of other people."

"My mother insisted that I take this assertiveness-training class, and I wasn't assertive enough to say no."

"I figure if I can't smell it, I won't eat it."

"Can't you see it, Cynthia? He's just using you!"

"[She] that always gives way to others will end in having no principles of [her] own." (Aesop.)

On Centering

Centering means checking in with yourself and shifting attention from external things to what's going on inside of you.

"Being centered is gathering the most complete, current, and accurate information about yourself. When I am centered, I know my own feelings, thoughts, choices, [and] wants, and I can draw on all my inner resources to meet challenges, solve problems, or make decisions." (The Phoenix Institute.)

"When I feel directed, aware, and balanced, I know that I am centered."

"I appreciate a man who's straightforward in his approach. I hope you appreciate a woman who's straightforward in her refusal!"

"A woman should be sure enough of herself to know the difference between focusing on others because she's interested and focusing on them for cues on how to behave."

"Just the other night I went to a wedding reception. I started feeling really insecure being in such an elegant place. Everyone was dressed beautifully and had gorgeously wrapped presents. I was dressed plainly and my present was home-wrapped, in this thin tissue, and you could see through it!

"I wanted to hide my present, and that's when I thought, 'This is silly. Why am I here?' I tried to center. I thought about how much I cared about these people. I realized I didn't have to be anything or prove anything. I just needed to be me." (A releasing pleaser.)

This woman changed her thoughts and took momentary charge of her self-esteem.

"Change your thoughts and you change your world." (Norman Vincent Peale.)

And she centered herself.

"When you start to center and get in touch with your physical, emotional, and spiritual being, and your mind is not out there doing a million things, you begin to direct your own life."

On Differentiating

In learning to center, the pleaser's challenge is to switch from an other-generated to a self-generated sense of worth.

"Women tend to center their lives around relationships and identify themselves in terms of those to whom they are connected." (Celia Halas and Roberta Matteson.)

"We give ourselves away constantly, in order to feel connected to others; it's as if we feared 'Death by Disconnection.'" (Sue Patton Thoele.)

A woman's central issue is developing a sense of self-worth that is minimally dependent upon other people's approval.

"Could she call you back? Right now she's on her 'pamper break.'"

"I embarrassed my son early one morning because I was out in the front yard in my nightgown picking roses off the rose bushes. He questioned, 'Mother, what if people see you?' And I said, 'What a wonderful thing to give them to talk about. So don't worry. Be happy!'"

"Just say, 'Oh well,' and smell the roses."

On Creating Self-Esteem

"Self-esteem is the ingredient for success, but it all depends on how you stir yourself."

"We have to learn to be our own best friends, because we fall too easily into the trap of being our worst enemies." (Roderick Thorp.)

"I have an inferiority complex, so I have to look out for number two."

"The trouble with inferiority complexes is that the right people don't have them." (Bill Leary.)

"No one can make you feel inferior without your consent." (Eleanor Roosevelt.)

"Don't say anything to yourself you wouldn't say to other people."

"Here's my best potion. It will make you love <u>yourself.</u>"

"I'm realizing that I'm just as good as people who are more important than I am."

"Lately, I've been feeling pretty adequate. Do you think I should see a therapist?"

On Firming Up the Self

"The real trouble comes with the need for the approval of everyone for every act. . . . [This] is tantamount to saying, 'Your view of me is more important than my own opinion of myself.'" (Wayne Dyer.)

"A [woman] cannot be comfortable without [her] own approval." (Mark Twain.)

"The central issue is not whether another judges you, but rather whether you accept that judgment." (Dorothy Corkille Briggs.)

"Accept good advice gracefully—as long as it doesn't interfere with what you intended to do in the first place." (Gene Brown.)

"OK, OK—your Boston cream pie doesn't need my advice!"

"Be yourself. No one can ever tell you you're doing it wrong." (James Leo Herlihy.)

"Be yourself. Who else is better qualified?" (Frank J. Giblin II.)

"Accept me as I am—only then will we discover each other."

"Every person has the right to be [herself], the person [she] is, the sum total of [her] feelings, thoughts, affections, tastes, dislikes and perceptions." (David Viscott.)

"If I am not for myself, who is for me?" (Hillel, Hebrew philosopher.)

"When I entered a room I used to think, 'What do these people think of me?' Now I think, 'What do I think of these people?'"

"You know what I like about you? When I need someone, you never turn your back on me!"

"It is not the end of the physical body that should worry us. Rather, our concern must be to *live* while we're alive—to release our inner selves from the spiritual death that comes with living behind a facade designed to conform to external definitions of who and what we are." (Elisabeth Kubler-Ross.)

"If you're going to create a firm self, make it downright hefty."

"I just made my own stock go up ten thousand points."

"Sorry. Yesterday was the deadline for all complaints."

On Trusting Self

"Refusing to have an opinion is a way of having one, isn't it?" (Luigi Pirandello.)

A woman needs to trust her own perceptions and judgments.

"Trust your hunches. . . . Hunches are usually based on facts filed away just below the conscious level." (Joyce Brothers, *How to Get Whatever You Want Out of Life.*)

*"George, we came here to get away from your
midlife crises—now sit down!"*

"Feminine intuition is a fiction and a fraud. It is nonsensical, illogical, emotional, ridiculous—and practically foolproof." (Harry Haenigsen.)

"Trust yourself. You know more than you think you do." (Benjamin Spock.)

"As soon as you trust yourself, you will know how to live." (Johann Wolfgang von Goethe.)

"I've decided to find out how to live."

"I used to be a debater before I was married, and lately I've felt like I have lost all my ability to analyze and to critique issues. I finally decided to do something. Now I listen to Oprah Winfrey and then mute the program and give my own opinion—while I'm ironing."

"For women, relying on their own perceptions is a new and exhilarating experience. . . . Learning that they can depend upon their own senses for accurate information about themselves builds a one-way bridge across the chasm separating self-doubt and effectiveness." (Celia Halas and Roberta Matteson.)

"You have to rid yourself of the feeling that you are somehow on the slave-trader's block and that someone has pinched your biceps and checked your teeth and found you wanting." (Penelope Russianoff.)

Or that you somehow have found your own self wanting. You can trust your self.

"When I want my husband's opinion, I give it to him."

"I'm the king, so we'll do it my way—is that all right with you, dear?"

"I'm going to start wearing a t-shirt that says, 'Everybody Is Entitled to My Opinion.'"

On Differences

"My view is not the same as yours, but that's okay."

"To disagree, one doesn't have to be disagreeable." (Barry M. Goldwater.)

"No two persons ever read the same book." (Edmund Wilson.)

"We all live under the same sky, but we don't have the same horizon." (Konrad Adenauer.)

"No two men are alike, and both of them are happy for it." (Morris Mandel.)

"What you dislike for yourself, do not like for me." (Spanish proverb.)

"Some people march to a different drummer—and some people polka."

"Have you tried sex?"

"Thoreau was no band leader. The sound of all those different drummers makes it hard to organize a parade." (David Gerrold.)

On Making Decisions

"Wonder how many fig leaves Eve tried on before she said, 'I'll take this one'?"

"I am positive, without a doubt, absolutely sure I am not indecisive anymore."

"She's like a puppy. When she can't make a decision she runs around in circles."

"I used to be indecisive, but now I'm not sure."

"Decision is a sharp knife that cuts clean and straight. Indecision is a dull one that hacks and tears and leaves ragged edges behind." (Jan McKeithen.)

"It's awful to be indecisive. You're like a centipede who's told to put his best foot forward."

"Standing in the middle of the road is very dangerous; you get knocked down by the traffic from both sides." (Margaret Thatcher.)

"To think too long about doing a thing often becomes its undoing." (Eva Young.)

"If you wait, all that happens is that you get older." (Larry McMurray.)

"Taking the bull by the horns is often a sound course of action—as long as you and the bull agree on when you can let go." (Robert Fuoss.)

"To make one good decision you have to
go through a lot of bad ideas."

"If you don't know what you really want to do, toss a coin. You suddenly know what you're hoping." (Madeline Lee.)

On Allowing Mistakes

"It is very easy to forgive others their mistakes; it takes more grit and gumption to forgive them for having witnessed your own." (Jessamyn West.)

"When I make mistakes, I always feel as if I'm what went wrong."

"I believed that I had a quirk deep inside that I had caused and that I had to correct before I could ever hope to be a viable human being."

"She's in there for making too many mistakes today."

"Failure is an event, never a person." (William D. Brown.)

Making mistakes is evidence of your humanity. You, like every other human being in this world, have the right to be wrong.

"I make mistakes; I'll be the second to admit it." (Jean Kerr.)

"The biggest mistake is clinging to past mistakes." (Dorothy Corkille Briggs.)

"Experience is a wonderful thing: it enables you to recognize a mistake every time you repeat it."

"If making mistakes was failure, then there would be no successes."

"I'm loyal to a fault. I've got a great many faults and I'm loyal to every one of them." (Steve Allen.)

"Always acknowledge a fault frankly. This will throw those in authority off their guard and give you opportunity to commit more." (Mark Twain.)

"Sorry, I forgot to warm up your side."

"I don't think life is about avoiding mistakes. I think it's about making them and coming to terms with them. . . . Playing safe is the worst thing anyone can do." (John Cleese.)

*"If you make the same mistake twice, that's part of the
learning curve—but three times is just dumb."*

"Compassion for myself is the most powerful healer of them all." (Theodore Isaac Rubin.)

"'Well adjusted' means you can make the same mistakes over and over again and keep smiling." (George Bergman.)

"Well adjusted" also means you can let *other people* make the same mistakes over and over again and keep smiling. It's vital to let other people make mistakes without penalty.

"Tact is rubbing out another's mistake instead of rubbing it in."

"Rare is the person who can weigh the faults of others without putting [her] thumb on the scales." (Byron J. Langenfield.)

On Tempering Anger

"Anger is a symptom, a way of cloaking and expressing feelings too awful to experience directly—hurt, bitterness, grief and, most of all, fear." (Joan Rivers.)

Women get angry when they "cave in" to keep peace:

"Anger is inevitable when our lives consist of giving in and going along; when we assume responsibility for other people's feelings and reactions; when we relinquish our primary responsibility to proceed with our own growth . . . ; when we behave as if having a relationship is more important than having a self." (Harriet Lerner.)

Giving up anger isn't easy.

"Helen, I wish you'd stop that!"

"My life is in the hands of any fool who makes me lose my temper." (Joseph Hunter.)

"It's hard to keep your shirt on when you're getting something off your chest." (Nipsey Russell.)

"Sometimes I wish my brain had call waiting."

"It is only our bad temper that we put down to being tired or worried or hungry; we put our good temper down to ourselves." (C. S. Lewis.)

"Nothing is as hard to do gracefully as getting down off your high horse." (Franklin P. Jones.)

"Getting angry can sometimes be like leaping into a wonderfully responsive sports car, gunning the motor, taking off at high speed and then discovering the brakes are out of order." (Maggie Scarf.)

"The end never justifies the meanness."

"Not the fastest horse can catch a word spoken in anger." (Chinese proverb.)

"If you are patient in one moment of anger, you will escape a hundred days of sorrow." (Chinese proverb.)

"Temper is a valuable possession—don't lose it."

"Wouldn't it be wonderful if, when we lost our temper, we couldn't ever find it again?"

On Representing Self

"Argue for your limitations, and sure enough, they're yours." (Richard Bach.)

The pleaser often feels that she isn't supposed to have needs.

"Many strong, capable women are merely complaining . . . rather than asking [men] for what they want." (Sue Browder.)

The pleaser's challenge is to represent her needs, wants, feelings, and opinions to others.

"You can't be afraid of stepping on toes if you want to go dancing." (Lewis Freedman.)

Still, you can watch where you put your "toes" . . .

In representing yourself, keep your fences mended and share your feelings or position without hostility or intent to retaliate. Aim to build, not destroy.

In representing your own needs, sometimes you need to "hang tough."

"I'm sorry, but this wall interferes with my getting to the copy machine!"

To represent yourself, claim ownership of your perceptions and your actions through "I" statements:

- I will . . .
- I choose . . .
- I want . . .
- I choose not . . .
- I accept . . .
- I hope . . .
- I wish . . .
- I need . . .
- I feel . . .

"You are the source and originator of all you think and feel." (Sherod Miller.)

Invite changes in others ("Would you be willing . . . ?") rather than make demands ("This is what you must do").

"Never claim as a right what you can ask as a favor." (John Churton Collin.)

"Do you want to make dinner—or shall I make reservations?"

"People usually get what's coming to them—unless it's been mailed."

You have a right to ask but no right to demand. If you demand, you may not get what you want, but you may get what you deserve.

"I thought you'd <u>never</u> get home!"

We do not own the property right to others.

Representing yourself means you accept your inalienable right to feel and think what you will, as long as you cause no harm.

"All of us could take a lesson from the weather. It pays no attention to criticism."

"Oh, oh . . ."

You can't please all the people all the time, so sometimes in life, you just have to please yourself.

*"Actually, our anniversary isn't for another three months—
but he doesn't know that!"*

"If you don't represent yourself, who will?"

Chapter 8

The Depleted Woman

Today's woman has gone "from superwoman to super-pooped." (Nicholas von Hoffman.)

"Having spent hours on her hands and knees stripping several layers of old wax from our kitchen floor, my wife was exhausted and sat down for a cup of coffee. Just then the kids came charging into the kitchen, hungry and anxious to eat. Reminding them how hard Mom had worked on the floor and how nice it looked, I added, 'Now if anyone spills anything on it, they first have to wipe it up and then spend an hour in their room.'

"Without hesitation, my wife deliberately poured some of her coffee on the floor, wiped it up, and headed straight upstairs. We didn't see her again for an hour." (Peter J. Larson.)

This is the depleted woman—that woman who runs on empty, who's too tired sometimes to even press the button on the hair spray.

"My pattern is go, go, go . . . collapse." (Rosie, as quoted by Anne Wilson Schaef.)

"The only energy I have left is static electricity."

"What an exhausting day! I spent three hours on hold!"

"My get-up-and-go has gotten up and went."

"I can either get ready to go or I can go, but I can't do both."

Despite her fatigue, the depleted woman keeps forging on.

"When I get up at night with the children, I keep my eyes half shut so I won't wake up too much."

"Nothing cures insomnia like the realization that it's time to get up."

"I wish I could think of a better way of starting the day than having to get up."

"What I need is a jumper cable."

"Or an alarm clock that won't ring."

"Or one that gives up."

"I get up in the morning and check the obituary column. If my name's not there, then I tell myself, 'I'd better get busy.'"

"My weekends are so awful that I feel as if the only thing that's holding me together is hair spray."

"On Mondays, I'm about as fit as a fizzle."

"My day was worse than your day!"

"Some days you win, some days you lose, but today I'd settle for a 7–10 split."

"I think they carry their arguments to extremes."

"My mother said there would be days like this, but she didn't tell me the whole truth."

The depleted woman operates on the edge.

"Sometimes I find myself muttering, 'Patience is a virtue and murder is a crime, and sometimes a cell all alone looks pretty good.'"

"Oh, hello, George. I pooped out somewhere between the kitchen and the living room."

And she's usually a grump.

"We're supposed to endure to the end—of what? Our patience?"

"Martha, please don't play 'our song' again."

The depleted woman pays a high price for doing too much too well.

"Fatigue is the most frequent health complaint among women." (Holly Atkinson.)

"I find by and large that women have to get sick to take care of themselves." (Marjorie Hansen Shaevitz.)

*"I wouldn't bother Mom if I were you.
She said she was 'too pooped for Pop'!"*

The depleted woman is putting her physical and emotional self in jeopardy and not paying attention. She has two choices:

"You can take care of yourself gracefully. Or you can take care of yourself ungracefully. But you *will* take care of yourself."

Taking care of yourself means taking care of your emotional and physical well-being, every day of your life for the rest of your life.

"With proper sleep, diet, and care, a healthy body will last a lifetime."

"The key to getting ahead is setting aside eight hours a day for work and eight hours a day for sleep—and making sure they're not the same hours." (Gene Brown.)

*"Mom, I can't sleep. Would you like to work
a little overtime and read me a bedtime story?"*

On Stress

Women need to learn to manage stress, which is probably the strongest contributing factor to lingering fatigue.

*"Isn't it wonderful? Everything that could go
wrong went wrong—and I didn't care!"*

"No noise is so emphatic as one you are trying not to listen to." (C. S. Lewis.)

"People who tell you never to let little things bother you have never tried sleeping in a room with a mosquito." (Katherine Chandler.)

"Sometimes the littlest things in life are the hardest to take. You can sit on a mountain more comfortably than on a tack."

"You may speak of love and tenderness and passion, but real ecstasy is discovering that you haven't lost your car keys after all." (Blackie Sherrod.)

"Stress builds up when the have-to's crowd out the want-to's."

"They didn't come to fix the dryer?"

"Too much stress is usually the result of a mismatch between your expectations and your environment. You can regain control by changing either one. Or sometimes you simply have to learn to flow rather than resist." (Robert S. Elliot.)

"Things will probably come out all right, but sometimes it takes strong nerves just to watch." (Hedley Donovan.)

"The only time I'm going to get my heartbeat up to 185 beats a minute is when I exercise. I'm not going to waste heartbeats on things I can't control."

"Looks like I owe you a 'for worse'!"

"One of the nicest things about problems is that a good many of them do not exist except in our imaginations." (Steve Allen.)

"I have known a great many troubles, but most of them never happened." (Mark Twain.)

"If you see ten troubles coming down the road, you can be sure that nine will run into the ditch before they reach you." (Calvin Coolidge.)

"If you treat every situation as a life-and-death matter, you'll die a lot of times." (Dean Smith.)

"If you can keep your head while all about you are losing theirs, you're probably not paying attention." (Franklin P. Jones.)

"Nonchalance is the ability to remain down to earth when everything else is up in the air." (Earl Wilson.)

"When you get to the end of your rope, tie a knot and hang on. And swing!" (Leo Buscaglia.)

"It happens every time she sees her monthly payroll!"

"Every stress survival kit should include a sense of humor."

"If you're going to be able to look back on something and laugh about it, you might as well laugh about it now." (Marie Osmond.)

"Patience is the ability to let your light shine after your fuse has blown." (Bob Levey.)

"The way I see it, if you want the rainbow, you've got to put up with the rain." (Dolly Parton.)

"If happiness truly consisted in physical ease and freedom from care, then the happiest individual would be neither a man nor a woman; it would be, I think, an American cow." (William Lyon Phelps.)

"Try to keep things in perspective. Fifty years from now, kids in history classes will be yawning over what panics us today."

"So, just don't get caught in the thick of thin things."

On Burnout

"I look at the stones in the cemetery when I drive by and think, 'That sure looks like an easy job.'"

"Sometimes I look at the obituary page in the newspaper and I feel jealous."

"The trouble with getting up is that every day begins with that first half hour of the morning."

"Cut that out!"

Burnout comes from chronic unrelieved stress, which leaves a woman overtired, overworked, and overloaded.

"Burnout is a state of physical, psychological, and sometimes spiritual exhaustion." (Joseph Procaccini, as quoted by Joan Libman.)

"It's when I feel tired, angry, and fed up with work. I'm less productive and I have no job loyalty."

"It's when the idea of shifting the laundry from the washer to the dryer seems like an impossible task."

"It's when I feel like I'll lose the synapses in my brain if I lean over."

To protect yourself from this kind of depletion, be alert for these burnout symptoms:

- a chronic energy slump
- crying jags and temper flareups
- headaches, insomnia, chest pains, stomach problems, colds
- mental fatigue, forgetfulness, difficulty concentrating
- a sense of entrapment and lack of control
- feeling driven, irritated, depleted, weary, worthless, and alone.

"I can sometimes spot women on the way to burnout. They sit straight and tall and look as if they feel they are the only ones dealing with the whole world." (Phyllis Smith, as quoted by Maggie Strong.)

Countering burnout requires facing it before it exacts a serious toll.

"A woman suffering from burnout typically feels that by *denying* the messages her body and mind are sending out, she will overcome the stresses and pressures of her life." (Herbert J. Fruedenberger and Gail North.)

Enduring fatigue is the body's signal that something is going wrong.

"Our body is our ally. When it sends warning signals, we need to reexamine our priorities and take action." (Peggy Stevens.)

"Come and prepare it!"

"You can maintain the balance between energy and demands by eliminating unproductive emotional drains and adding self-replenishing activities." (Carol Tannenhauser.)

"I'm still going to charge you for a regular office visit!"

On Clinical Depression

"On staring out at a gloomy day: First you must realize that it is the day that is gloomy, not you. If you want to be gloomy, too, that's all right, but it's not mandatory." (Nora Gallagher.)

This woman is talking about "depression-the-blues." Every woman has blue moods at times, caused by real events in her life. But the moods don't linger.

"When I found myself crying over the drought in Kansas, I realized it was a wake-up call."

If a woman can't control her mood—if she is down much or all of the time or if she is having major mood swings—she likely has clinical or chemical depression.

"It's like a prison you can't escape. It's in your head, always haunting you."

"It's too bad our skins don't turn green when we get depressed. Then we'd get the help we need."

"The 'average' woman today stands a shocking 25 percent chance of experiencing a major depression in her lifetime; and, overall, professional women are three to five times more likely to attempt suicide than nonprofessional women." (Anne McCammon.)

Clinical depression includes all of burnout's symptoms in intense and chronic form, plus—

- loss of self-esteem and self-confidence
- overeating or undereating
- loss of sexual desire (or extremely high sexual drive)
- irritability, angry outbursts
- anxiety, worry, and nervousness
- loss of pleasure and sense of humor
- self-neglect
- isolation, withdrawal
- feelings of hopelessness and helplessness
- suicidal thinking

"Depression is more than a lack of energy; it is a mood disorder that affects one's entire outlook on life and physical well-being." (Holly Atkinson.)

Clinical depression is a *physical* disorder (like ulcers or diabetes) caused by abnormalities in the neurotransmitters, or chemicals, in the brain. These chemicals conduct the electrical impulses which allow clear thinking, mood elevation, and a sense of well-being.

Clinical depression is not just an inability to deal with life's challenges. Women with clinical depression have a chronic illness, just as do women with diabetes or arthritis.

Depression often results when a woman is bombarded by too much stress or too many changes in too short a time, overwhelming her capacity to cope.

"Depression can . . . be generated by feeling hopelessly entrenched in paralyzing situations over which one has no control and is powerless to change." (Celia Halas and Roberta Matteson.)

Clinical depression can also occur with childbirth.

"About 12 percent of all women who give birth are likely to suffer postpartum depression." (Michael O'Hara.)

"These are women who are overcome with sadness, who stare at the breakfast dishes and wonder how they will ever have the energy to wash them, who sometimes feel suicidal, who can't sleep or who want to sleep all the time, who are fidgety with anxiety, who sometimes begin to hate their newborns." (Elaine Jarvik.)

Depression can creep up on a woman in midlife, as she becomes less physically active and her ovaries produce less estrogen in the early stages of menopause. In midlife, depression is a major risk factor in divorce, with a woman often abandoning a marriage that she views through clouded lenses. As menopause approaches, depression symptoms such as low stress tolerance, increased anger, numbness, confusion, and withdrawal can lead a woman to eliminate the stress closest to her—her mate—who she feels is at the root of her problems.

"Very often a change of self is needed more than a change of scene." (A. C. Benson.)

Finally, a woman may suffer from a genetic bipolar disorder that is exacerbated by aging, stress, and childbirth. Various configurations of symptoms may include depression, "flash" anger, anxiety, or euphoria in intense or muted form. Pressured speech, distractability, impulsivity, and wide mood swings are often present.

"I always walked on emotional quicksand. I could never trust my own feelings or judgment."

In today's world, with appropriate medical help, no woman needs to suffer the debilitating effects of a chemical disorder.

"Anti-depressant . . . anti-depressant . . . anti . . ."

"Once I grew well I had a blinding vision of waste—of people's lives grinding down beneath depressions that can be cured, if only they knew." (Anne McCammon.)

On Women, Men, Fatigue, and Intimacy

"Most [working] women without children spend more time than [their husbands] on housework; with children, they devote more time to both housework and child care. . . . Most women work one shift at the office or factory and a 'second shift' at home." (Arlie Hochschild.)

"Yes, my husband is a great help around the house. Right now he's taking the baby's nap for him." (Leo Aikman.)

Occasionally a woman may view a husband as seeing the world through her eyes but just not caring enough about her plight. She's going down for the third time and he doesn't even throw her a life preserver. She carries around a chronic low burn toward this man.

"Sometimes I wonder if men and women really suit each other. Perhaps they should live next door and just visit now and then." (Katharine Hepburn.)

"Of course you have <u>nothing</u> to do . . . you've already <u>done</u> it!"

"I know that we men still don't do enough housework, but now we feel guilty about it." (An informed '90s man.)

"Men don't see cobwebs. It's not in their genes."

"Most fights over women's rights take place in the family kitchen, not the state capitol." (Francine and Douglas Hall, as quoted by Carol Krucoff.)

"In my experience most men cannot find in their *own* kitchens what most women can find in a stranger's kitchen." (Letty Cottin Pogrebin.)

"I finally asked my husband who he thought did the dishes—the dish fairy?"

"My husband seems to believe in a Great Sock Fairy."

"I do things she never notices, too. When she goes on about the Sock Fairy I say, 'What about the Fuel Fairy who puts gas in the car?'"

"Our interviews revealed that women feel angry and men feel underappreciated." (Laura Lein.)

When I said 'I do,' it didn't mean I would do everything!"

Both sexes are fighting about chores, but what really presses and aggravates both men and women are sweeping gender-role changes that are calling into question what once were cut-and-dried traditional role definitions.

"My guess is that women will continue to expect more

help and men will give more, but that will take a restructuring of work and home roles. That will take, oh, about two hundred years." (Ethel Klein.)

"We call men the opposite sex, because when we ask them to do something, they do the opposite."

"The way to get a man to help with the laundry is to tell him that men who help have longer-lasting marriages." (Larry Tritten.)

For most women, there is a "sex and housework" connection. Men don't know that women associate love with a man's willingness to help. A man doesn't have a clue about the connection because he associates having a house with being nurtured, not with doing housework. He wonders why his wife is so resentful.

"Do you want to talk about it?"

"If you want a better marriage, don't think of your participation in housework as 'helping'—think of housework as half yours." (Another informed '90s man.)

"If we men only knew how much women would respect our sincere attempts at domestic competence, we would all be down on our knees scrubbing the floor instead of puttering around at the office." (Frank Pittman.)

"Tonight I'm taking you out to dinner after I wash, iron, and clean house—but first I'm going to make mad, passionate love to you—April Fool's!"

A woman who is juggling home, family, and possibly a job, adding more and more to her schedule without deleting much, is an overloaded, overworked, and overstressed woman. She's also a woman who won't be very interested in sexual intimacy.

"My sex life is little more than a fond memory." (Barbara J. Berg.)

When exhausted, women are too tired for sexual intimacy, but men who are tired aren't. They say, "I'm tired, but not *too* tired . . . "

"I don't get it. You were too tired to help me around the house, and now, all of a sudden, you're not too tired for <u>that</u>?"

"Men's sexual desire simply is not affected by fatigue in the way a woman's is. A husband may be tired and yet still hunger for sex, while his tired wife hungers for nothing but sleep." (Roberta Markowitz.)

Unlike a man, Roberta Markowitz notes, a woman who succumbs to exhaustion is affected by a delicate interplay of both emotional and physical factors. She often experiences physical touch as intrusive and overstimulating when her brain is already overwhelmed with sensory overload. As a result, she shuts down.

"The best thing you can say about the average working mother's sex life is that it's not time-consuming." (Hester Mundis.)

The answer to this disconcerting state of affairs? Men need to help more, and women need to get more sleep.

Chapter 9

Women and Health

Be careful about reading health books. You might die of a misprint." (Mark Twain.)

"The only way to stay healthy is to exercise—do a little skipping. Like skip smoking, skip drinking, skip rich foods." (Bill Kennedy.)

"The only way to keep your health is to eat what you don't want, drink what you don't like, and do what you'd druther not." (Mark Twain.)

*"It all started when I was a little girl with my mother
constantly yelling, 'Eat it! It's good for you.'"*

On Diet

Most women can relate to the "stress diet":

Breakfast:
1/2 grapefruit
1 piece whole wheat bread (toasted)
8 oz. skim milk

Lunch:
4 oz. lean broiled chicken breast
1 cup steamed zucchini
1 Oreo cookie
herb tea

Midafternoon snack:
rest of package of Oreo cookies
1 quart rocky road ice cream
1 jar hot fudge

Dinner:
2 loaves garlic bread
large mushroom and pepperoni pizza
1 large chocolate almond caramel cashew shake
3 Milky Ways
Entire frozen cheesecake (eaten directly from freezer)

The question, of course, is whether this or any other diet *relieves* or *causes* stress.

What really causes stress is the new pasta diet: "Just walk pasta bakery without stopping. Walk pasta candy store without stopping. Walk pasta ice-cream shop without stopping." (*Optimist Magazine,* as quoted in *Reader's Digest.*)

"A diet is questioning whether thin people really do have more fun." (Bill Adler.)

"A diet is a plan for putting off tomorrow what you put on today." (Ivern Ball.)

"A diet is serving your skinny friends fudge cake while you eat an apple." (Bill Adler.)

"The toughest part of dieting isn't watching what you eat; it's watching what your friends eat." (Wilfred Beaver.)

"It's just that every time I lose the cordless phone,
I find it in the refrigerator."

"Probably nothing in the world arouses more false hopes than the first four hours of a diet." (Dan Bennett.)

"There's one thing to be said for a diet—it certainly does improve your appetite." (Earl Wilson.)

"We never repent of having eaten too little." (Thomas Jefferson.)

"A diet is something you go on . . . to go off! Don't go on anything that you're not willing (or able) to stay on forever." (Jane Brody.)

"If I can't diet, what will I have to suffer over?"

"You can join the 'fight against hazardous waists.'"

On a Lifestyle Change

"What is needed is a lifestyle change—learning to eat three or more sensible meals a day, with wholesome snacks and occasional no-nos and plenty of satisfying complex carbohydrates, and making exercise as routine a part of your life as brushing your teeth." (Jane Brody.)

In addition to adding complex carbohydrates, a lifestyle change means making a hit list of high-fat foods to stay away from, snacking sensibly, and satisfying your sweet tooth wisely.

"There are two times when a closed mouth can be of help to you—when you're about to say something against a person, and when you're offered dessert." (O. A. Battista.)

"When I told him I was starved for love,
he bought me more chocolates."

Why go for a lifestyle change—of eating, sleeping, and exercising well? Because you're worth it. You'll live longer and better and be more energetic.

"I decided to make a lifestyle change, but only for short periods, maybe fifteen or twenty minutes at a time, and mostly in between meals."

"A lot of us have seen the light, but for many of us it's the one inside of the refrigerator." (Marlys Huffman.)

"If you consider yourself at least as important as a houseplant that will die without sun, food and water, you'll pay attention to your own care and feeding." (Denise Foley.)

You know it's time for a change in lifestyle when you push away from the table and the table moves.

Or when you look in a three-way mirror.

"Or when you're wearing a red, white, and blue dress, you're on the street corner yawning, and someone drops a letter in your mouth." (Phyllis Diller.)

"I could lose weight far easier if replacement parts weren't so handy in the refrigerator."

"I don't want to hurt your feelings, but some of you HAS to go!"

"I'm not going to eat any more double-fudge cake. It makes my clothes shrink."

"I love the permanent weight-loss class. I take it year after year."

On Exercise

"Exercise is our friend." (Kelley Garrett.)

"My idea of exercise is a good brisk sit!" (Phyllis Diller.)

"The first time I see a jogger smiling, I'll consider trying it." (Joan Rivers.)

"I do 20 sit-ups every morning, but it wears me out to hit the snooze alarm so many times." (J. Scott Homan.)

"For my birthday, my husband upgraded my barbells."

*"Actually, it was an easy day at the office.
I look like this because of my aerobics class!"*

"I began walking a mile a day, but all I lost was two inches—off the bottom of my tennis shoes."

"If it weren't for the fact that the TV set and the refrigerator are so far apart, some of us wouldn't get any exercise at all." (Joey Adams.)

"Exercise used to be such a dirty word that every time I thought about it I had to wash my mouth out with a chocolate."

"The first time I exercised, I listened to my body, but I didn't like what it said."

"I'm doing all this cross-training, and all I get is cross."

*"Patience, Harold. Three more miles and I'll
have reached Brisbane, Australia."*

"I'm finally benefiting from all the exercising I'm doing.
I'm getting aches, pains, stiffness, and fatigue."

*"OK, everyone, clear the room—
I've got to lie on the floor and zip up my pants."*

"I'm getting so good I can do a seventy-minute exercise
videotape in just twenty minutes simply by fast-forwarding it."

On the Benefits of Exercise

"If a miracle drug came on the market to reduce your fatigue, increase your energy, speed up your metabolism, and help you lose weight, would you take it? What if it also improved your mood, slowed aging, decreased your risk of illness, and prolonged your life—without negative side effects?" (Holly Atkinson.)

What if this miracle drug even reduced your chances of developing cancer, heart disease, and osteoporosis and had a beneficial effect on cardiovascular fitness, muscle strength, bone density, flexibility, coordination, and alertness?

The miracle drug, of course, is exercise. What more could we ask for?

"Women who want a sense of mastery over their lives may often gain it through exercise. They understand the link between energizing their bodies and invigorating their minds." (Robert S. Brown, M.D., as quoted in "Self Survey.")

Make daily appointments with yourself to exercise, and then keep those appointments, just as you would with any other important person.

On Breast Exams

"The single greatest risk factor for getting breast cancer is being a woman." (National expert in women's health.)

One in nine women will develop breast cancer in her lifetime. Every three minutes, a woman in the United States learns she has breast cancer. In 1992 there were 180,000 new cases of breast cancer. Forty-six thousand of those women died.

If every woman examined her breasts monthly and got tested at the recommended intervals, 15,000 lives a year could be saved.

"If a child needed a trip to heaven and back, a woman would try to arrange that trip, but for heaven's sake, if you tell her she has a one in nine chance of getting breast cancer and that the best way to find this cancer early is through monthly self-examinations of her breasts, she doesn't do it." (Valerie Logston, M.D.)

Today an estimated 1.5 million women in the United States are living after bouts with breast cancer. They are the lucky ones. Or the smart ones who, through monthly breast exams or periodic mammograms, found a lump in time.

Make a commitment to yourself to do monthly breast examinations. Vigilance is key to early detection of breast cancer.

*"There are three things you have to remember
about being a woman: exercise, get a good education,
and do regular breast self-examinations."*

Many major health organizations now recommend mammography every five years for women between ages eighteen and forty; every two years for women between ages forty-one and fifty; and every year for women over fifty. Erma Bombeck, a survivor of breast cancer, offers hope to other survivors:

"Women are not appliances that come with lifetime guarantees, to be discounted when a part breaks. . . . Without a breast, I still form coherent sentences and intelligent opinions. I defy anyone to tell me which of my columns were written by a single-breasted writer."

There is, she assures, life after breast cancer.

On Smoking

Breast cancer in women is secondary only to lung cancer.

"In the past thirty-five years, lung cancer has gone from being the lowest cause of cancer death in women to the highest." (A cancer researcher.)

"By the time lung cancer is diagnosed, it's often too late for curative treatment." (Another cancer researcher.)

Further, "smoking is the most important controllable risk factor for heart attack. Studies show that smoking one to four cigarettes daily doubles the risk. Smoking more than twenty-five a day raises it five to fifteen times the risk."

"About the only beneficial thing in smoking is that it repels gnats and mosquitoes. Which only proves you don't have to be big to be smart." (Paul Sweeney.)

"It's easy to stop smoking; I've done it thousands of times." (Mark Twain.)

"If at first you don't succeed, quit and quit again."

Chapter 10

Women and Appearance

Many women equate what they look like with who they are.

"When someone asks me how I am, I tell them how I look instead of how I feel."

"Like every other woman, I stand in front of the mirror with nine thousand outfits every morning before I find the right one." (Donna Karan.)

"Take all the time you need to frame your response."

"I never forget that a woman's first job is to choose the right shade of lipstick." (Carole Lombard.)

"A man may keep his nose to the grindstone, but a woman had better stop now and again to powder hers." (Susan Brownmiller.)

"It's an ill wind that blows the minute you leave the hairdresser." (Phyllis Diller.)

"If only your hairdresser knows for sure, you get to the beauty parlor a lot more often than I do."

Most women invest heavily in cosmetics to make themselves more appealing to *themselves*.

"What I really need is an industrial-strength moisturizer."

"I found a new skin-care cream that gently and safely removes forty dollars."

*"We have a dinner engagement at the Carlsons' in three days—
I'm going to start putting on my makeup!"*

"I think what I need is a magician, not a beautician."

"Nobody ever died from a bad haircut, but many a woman has wanted to." (Maggie Scarf.)

"Women end up feeling ashamed when caught unadorned." (Rita Freedman.)

And women invest in external trappings . . .

"How I hate shoulder pads! I have ripped enough of

them out of my own clothes to pad my own cell." (Erma Bombeck.)

"There's no problem finding the right pair—one size hurts all."

"I have what I call a stock-exchange dress—when I hit 130, it splits." (Connie Stevens.)

"I design my clothes for the reason that I know better than anyone what I have to hide." (Vera Stravinsky.)

Women need to quit relying on "plastic surgery" every morning to make themselves beautiful.

"I'm tired of all this nonsense about beauty being only skin deep. That's enough. What do you want, an adorable pancreas?" (Jean Kerr.)

And instead, they need to embrace their inner cores.

"Over the years I have learned that what is important in a dress is the woman who is wearing it." (Yves Saint Laurent.)

"Hi! You're so nice to come home to!"

"A winning smile is the best accessory any dress ever had." (C. Terry Cline, Jr.)

"Taking joy in living is a woman's best cosmetic." (Rosalind Russell.)

On Body Image

Most women spend their lives trying to achieve the Body Perfect and always berate themselves because they come up short.

"She had an hourglass figure—but time stood still in the wrong places." (Aaron Gold.)

"She has an hourglass figure, but all the sand is at the bottom."

"I have an awful body—even my mirror won't look back."

"Whatever the biological components of beauty, it is culture that confers meaning on them." (Rita Freedman.)

"It doesn't take more than five minutes watching network television or flipping through a magazine to see what our society considers the ideal of feminine beauty: wrinkle-free and model-thin for starters." (Ellen Sue Stern.)

"The fact is that nearly every female is 'flawed' in some way, and it's only the woman without flaws who is the freak." (Anne Bernays.)

"I remember thinking, 'I'm just a worthless person. I'll be fat like this forever. This will never come off.'"

"Our only crime—aside from the occasional Oreo lapse—is being human. Vulnerability should inspire compassion, not contempt. We deserve better from ourselves." (Gloria Nagy.)

"My darling girl, please don't try to be perfect—the *defect* is very important." (Italian director Vittorio de Sica to Raquel Welch.)

"We are so busy obsessing over what is wrong with us— whether it's our weight, misproportion, wrinkles, pimples, excess hair, or functional limitations—that we fail to develop our potential as human beings." (Marcia Germaine Hutchinson.)

"My nose is too long. My ears protrude. My chin is receding.
My tail's too short. My complexion is scaly. I'm a mass
of wrinkles, and I sag all over."

We can all stretch the boundaries of beauty to "make room for the stouter, older, plainer, flatter, freckled, and funny-faced among us. Simply by reinforcing others for non-conventional beauty choices, we can alter the norm." (Rita Freedman.)

"Face it, Lisa! You just don't have a designer body!"

Stretching those boundaries includes accepting ourselves as we grow older:

"I don't have wrinkles. I just have more detail than most."

We need to accept our overall body image as well:

"I've made a new truce with my body: As long as I exercise enough to stay healthy and look reasonably nice in clothes, that's Personally Good Enough." (Jeanie Wilson.)

On Comparing

Women often feel that their appearance makes a presentation to the world, and they compare themselves to other women who are also making presentations:

"I went to the grocery store the other day with wilted hair, no makeup, and in my sweats. I said to myself, 'No one will notice me in my disguise.' Then I realized that the other me—the one who dresses up and takes half a morning to do her hair and makeup—is really the woman in disguise."

Women habitually compare characteristics in themselves to the random and enviable characteristics of any woman who crosses their path.

"She's so thin, and here I've worked out for a year and I'm still not where I want to be. It must have been all that licorice I ate."

Then they compare their insides—their hidden faults and flaws—with other women's outsides.

"You can always find someone who is thinner, brighter, richer, more organized than you are."

"Comparing yourself with others is disrespectful to yourself."

"When we compare ourselves, we don't do it with one whole person against one whole person. It's with ten people, and we have to be the best of all ten of them."

"Probably no habit chips away at our self-confidence quite so effectively as that of scanning the people around us to see how we compare." (Alan Loy McGinnis.)

"Since God made us to be originals, why stoop to be a copy?" (Billy Graham.)

"Don't compare yourself with anyone else. Forget all about the position of others. Measure yourself on what you have done, what you are doing, and what you can do. You are in a race with yourself and your own possibilities. Let what you do today compete with and surpass what you did yesterday." (William J. Reilly.)

"You're a thoroughbred, and thoroughbreds don't watch other horses; they run their own race." (Danny Thomas to daughter Marlo.)

Remember: You're a thoroughbred, too.

On Accepting Compliments

Women tend to usher in any negatives and suffer over them.

"You're always wearing a new outfit! Do you spend all your money on clothes?"

They accept willingly any unearned criticism but deflect applause that comes to them.

"You should see me in the morning without my makeup."

"I'd really look better if I was ten pounds lighter."

It would be fairer to accept positives and deflect negatives. Just accept a compliment gracefully with a smile and say, "Thank you very much."

Then let that compliment in. Feel it. Savor it. Experience its warmth. Treat yourself to the good feeling you're entitled to that springs from being validated by someone who recognizes your strengths and possibilities.

Chapter 11

Investing in Yourself

Every woman needs a self-enhancement, repair, and maintenance program. You are your own guardian and taskmaster.

"I don't know whether to be sad that you're all going to leave the nest someday or happy to have the bathroom all to myself!"

On Selfing

"People often say that this or that person has not yet found himself. But the self is not something that one finds. It is something one creates." (Thomas Szasz.)

"It's just that I've never seen you without your makeup before."

"Everyone in life has been given certain puzzle pieces. We're all trying to put together the same puzzle and it is called the Self. I'm given a few pieces, and another person is given a few pieces. We're all different, but the pieces are a lot alike." (Debbie Barmonde.)

"One of the labors of adulthood is to befriend in ourselves those handicapped and underdeveloped parts of our nature which we have set aside." (M. C. Richards.)

"You are the gift you give yourself." (Richard L. Evans.)

On Becoming a Whole Person

When women merge with men at the expense of having a self, they can pay an exorbitant price.

"Their other-generated sense of themselves is dependent upon the successes and failures of their husbands and children." (Celia Halas and Roberta Matteson.)

In giving service, the woman often wears herself out, neglecting to save a piece of her for herself.

"I thought for years and years that the more I did for other people, the more I sacrificed myself, the better mother, wife, or daughter I was, the better I would feel about myself. It hasn't turned out that way. I just feel empty. Somewhere, I lost me."

As long as a woman continues to postpone living her own life, waiting to be endorsed with a stamp of approval of another, her "self" is on hold.

"I finally decided to give myself permission to have an identity and something more than clean cupboards."

"Every one of us has in him a continent of undiscovered character. Blessed is he who acts the Columbus of his own soul."

"Remember, I'm Mrs. Marge Bentley, the woman and partner in our marriage—this is your faithful companion."

"As my own guardian, I took charge of creating my 'self.'"

On Personal Value

You are intrinsically valuable simply because you *are.*

"What we must decide is how we are valuable rather than how valuable we are." (Edgar Z. Friedenberg.)

"What do you mean, 'It will pay for itself'?
Who has been paying for me?"

There are no carbon copies. You are an unprecedented event in the universe.

"Another thing that happens once in a lifetime is you." (Tony Pettito.)

As a self, you are similar to the stunning and one-of-a-kind pictures created by a turn of the crystals in a kaleidoscope.

"Your self-worth . . . must be unrelated to your self-assessments. You exist. You are human. That is all you need. Your worth is determined by you, and with no need for an explanation to anyone. And your worthiness, a given, has nothing to do with your behavior and feelings." (Wayne Dyer.)

"We relish news of our heroes, forgetting that we are extraordinary, too." (Helen Hayes.)

"Take good care of yourself—you belong to me."

On Growth

As forever-evolving beings, we are always in process and in pursuit of our own growth.

"What we are is God's gift to us. What we become is our gift to God." (Eleanor Powell.)

"Nature does not demand that we be perfect. It requires only that we grow." (Joshua Loch Liehman.)

"You mean as a woman I have to keep growing?"

"We work to become, not to acquire." (Elbert Hubbard.)

"We cannot become what we need to be by remaining what we are." (Max De Pere.)

But sometimes we inadvertently stop ourselves from fulfilling our potential and leading out in quest of our own growth.

Can't and *won't* are contractions of two different verbs. *Can't* means precisely that—"I can't"—but *won't* means "I choose not to." I've learned that I have to act on my own behalf.

There is a stark difference between asking permission and coordinating.

"I've waited all my life for permission to do what I wanted. Now I realize that I don't need permission—I just need courage."

"Mom, whose permission do I need to become a woman?"

"Always try to live a little bit beyond your capacities, and you'll find your capacities are greater than you ever dreamed." (Arthur Gordon.)

"If you are willing to be the person you were meant to be, I think you will discover that for you the sky is the limit." (Ted Engstrom.)

"Use what talents you possess; the woods would be very

silent if no birds sang there except those that sang best."
(Henry Van Dyke.)

"We don't know who we are until we see what we can
do." (Martha Grimes.)

"I have never known a woman who, having embraced
the best within herself, later expressed regret at having done
so. But I have known many women who, having avoided
this choice, sentenced themselves to a lifetime of regret."
(Nathaniel Branden.)

"If I live my life the way you want me to, then it's no longer my life!"

On Taking Charge

"Am I dumb! My closet had toilet cleaners, detergents, mops,
brooms, and a vacuum cleaner—his had a golf bag!"

"If you want to change something, do something different; and occasionally, listen to your mother." (A *Cathy* cartoon by Cathy Guisewite.)

"I wondered why somebody didn't do something. Then I realized I was somebody." (Letter to "Dear Abby.")

The challenge is to become the best you can be. You can be in charge of how your life will play out.

"The important thing about your lot in life is whether you use it for building or parking."

"The biggest mistake you can make is to believe you're working for someone else."

"Do not let what you cannot do interfere with what you can do." (John Wooden.)

Only you can make your life more interesting, more rewarding, more satisfying.

*"I see fame in your future. Someday
they'll name a syndrome after you."*

So go for your dreams. You're worth the time, energy, and resources it takes.

"Life is uncharted territory. It reveals its story one moment at a time." (Leo Buscaglia.)

"Every person's life is worth a novel. . . . People are often the last ones to recognize the drama in their own lives. They marvel at the adventure of others but don't look inside

to see that their own lives hold just as much possibility."
(Erving Polster.)

"Few of us live beyond our three score and ten years and
yet in that brief time most of us create and live a unique
biography and weave ourselves into the fabric of human history." (Elisabeth Kubler-Ross.)

"We must overcome the notion that we must be regular.
. . . It robs you of the chance to be extraordinary and leads
you to the mediocre." (Uta Hagen.)

"Be bold in what you stand for and careful what you fall
for." (Ruth Boorstin.)

"Whatever you can do, or dream you can, begin it.
Boldness has genius, power, and magic in it." (Goethe.)

"Be bold, and mighty forces will come to your aid."
(Basic King.)

"Life shrinks or expands in proportion to one's courage."

"If you risk nothing, then you risk everything." (Geena
Davis.)

"It is not because things are difficult that we do not dare;
it is because we do not dare that they are difficult." (Seneca.)

"Take a chance! All life is a chance. The [woman] who
goes furthest is generally the one who is willing to do and
dare." (Dale Carnegie's Scrapbook.)

"All serious daring starts from within." (Eudora Weitz.)

"Far away is far away only if you don't go there."
(O Povo.)

"Go wherever you have always wanted to go. Go as
soon as you can, for as far as you can, for as long as you
can."

"If your ship doesn't come in, swim out to it!" (Jonathan
Winters.)

"If you don't make waves, you're not under way."
(Leonard P. Gollobin.)

"We need to learn to set our course by the stars, not by
the lights of every passing ship." (Omar Bradley.)

The first thing Marjorie Winthrop learned in night school
was how to delegate responsibility.

"It is not the lofty sails but the unseen wind that moves the ship." (W. Mac Neile Dixon.)

"I can't change the direction of the wind, but I can adjust my sails to always reach my destination." (Jimmy Dean.)

"Ideals are like the stars. We never reach them, but like the mariners on the sea, we chart our course by them." (Carl Schurtz.)

"When you reach for the stars, you may not quite get one, but you won't come up with a handful of mud either." (Leo Burnett.)

"The winds and waves are always on the side of the ablest navigators." (Edward Gibbon.)

"Start by doing what's necessary, then what's possible, and suddenly you are doing the impossible." (St. Francis of Assisi.)

On Goals

"Having the world's best idea will do you no good unless you act on it. People who want milk shouldn't sit on a stool in the middle of a field in hopes that a cow will back up to them." (Curtis Grant.)

"The trouble with not having a goal is that you can

spend your life running up and down the field and never scoring." (Bill Copeland.)

"Goals determine what you're going to be." (Julie Erving.)

"A woman with a contractor's license can move any mountain."

"Do not cut loose from your longings, for what are we without our longings?" (Amos Oz.)

"Everything starts as somebody's daydream." (Larry Niven.)

"A wish is a desire without an attempt." (*Farmer's Digest.*)

"Few wishes come true by themselves." (June Smith.)

"The best way to make your dreams come true is to wake up." (J. M. Power.)

"Goals are dreams with deadlines." (Diana Scharf Hunt.)

"Dreams and dedication are a powerful combination." (William Longgood.)

"Whoever wants to reach a distant goal must take many small steps." (Helmut Schmidt.)

"Be like a postage stamp—stick to one thing until you get there." (Josh Billings.)

"Any last words before we seal this commitment for eternity?"

On Education

"A man was out walking in the desert when a voice said to him, 'Pick up some pebbles and put them in your pocket, and tomorrow you will be both sorry and glad.'

"The man obeyed. He stooped down and picked up a handful of pebbles and put them in his pocket. The next morning he reached into his pocket and found diamonds and rubies and emeralds. And he was both glad and sorry. Glad that he had taken some—sorry he hadn't taken more.

"And so it is with education." (William Cunningham.)

"Thank goodness I took that night course in business administration."

In today's world, an education is as available to you as your commitment to it.

"Education is about the only thing lying around loose in the world, and it's about the only thing a fellow can have as much of as he's willing to haul away." (George Horace Lorimer.)

In the '90s, women are finding their strength through education.

"The world stands aside to let anyone pass who knows where she is going."

"I have never let my schooling interfere with my education." (Mark Twain.)

"Education is the ability to listen to almost anything without losing your temper or your self-confidence." (Robert Frost.)

"The best-educated human being is the one who understands most about the life in which [she] is placed." (Helen Keller.)

"Mother! Doing your homework with the TV on?!"

"The trouble is, I have to show my report card to my kids."

On Learning

"Learning is not attained by chance. It must be sought for with ardor and attended to with diligence." (Abigail Adams.)

Learning is more than a luxury; it is a responsibility you owe to yourself.

"The real learning process begins the day you realize you have to learn."

"Learning isn't a means to an end; it is an end in itself." (Robert A. Heinlein.)

"The best of all things is to learn. Money can be lost or stolen, health and strength may fail, but what you have committed to your mind is yours forever." (Louis L'Amour.)

In the process of learning, you give yourself the gift of new eyes.

"The real voyage of discovery consists not in seeking new lands, but of seeing with new eyes." (Marcel Proust.)

"Nobody has ever thought [herself] to death." (Gilbert Highet.)

And you give yourself a sense of empowerment and mastery.

"There is a growing strength in women, but it's in the forehead, not in the forearm." (Beverly Sills.)

And you gain an infusion of new ideas to energize your relationships.

"[Learning] is not training but rather the process that equips you to entertain yourself, a friend, and an idea." (Wallace Sterling.)

"The chili really packs a wallop, doesn't it, dear?"

And you get positive feedback.

"Every time I get an 'A' paper at school, my kids want to put it on the refrigerator. They're tickled pink."

"With my kids learning at school all day, I realized, 'Why shouldn't I?'"

As a bonus, you become far more interesting to yourself.

Taking on a commitment to learning at any age, of course, often requires a balancing act.

"I was going to do my homework last night, but my husband put me to bed early." (Erma Bombeck.)

And commitment requires an investment of time. Don't wait until you have enough time or you'll be like this poor woman:

"All I ever really wanted to do was paint, but I was waiting until the children were grown and I had enough time. Then my husband died and I had to go to work, so I was waiting until I retired and had enough time. But now that I'm retired, my hands are so arthritic I can't hold a brush, so now I'm waiting till I get to heaven." (Jo Coudert.)

"When I got to heaven, I thought, 'At last I can do what I always wanted to do!' But there are no typewriters, no word processors, no paper, no pencils, no crayons, no . . ."

The moral is: Invest in yourself in ways that make sense—now, not later—and certainly before you get to heaven!

Chapter 12

A Personal Credo for Enhancing Self-Esteem

I embrace the position that I am an intrinsically valuable human being. I am a worthy person simply because I am.

I separate my behavior from my person. I realize there will always be changes I can make to improve myself. However, these changes have to do with my growth, not my worth.

I understand that making mistakes also has to do with growth, not worth. I give myself permission to make mistakes and still be okay. I also release myself from past mistakes, recognizing that I cannot risk or grow without making errors.

I realize that some of my greatest learning has come from mistakes I have made.

I expect at times I will incur the disapproval of others. I recognize there is no way I can please all the people all the time.

I realize that disapproval comes from imperfect people, like myself, who often change moods, easily become critical, and readily strike out and label others when they themselves are hurting. Because I cannot control such disapproval, I refuse to reduce my self-worth when I encounter others' irritation, anger, or harsh words.

I understand that others have choices in the way they offer feedback. If they choose to belittle or lash out rather than offer constructive help, I realize their destructive behavior has to do with them, not me.

I will search the messages of others for information helpful to my growth process, but I refuse to give credence to criticism from those who do not have my best interests at heart.

I give my self-assessment priority over the assessment of others, but here I will be fair, acknowledging assets as well as liabilities.

I release myself from concentrating on my shortcomings. Rather than searching relentlessly for my flaws, I will search relentlessly for my strengths.

I will nurture myself by giving approving, accepting, reassuring messages to myself about me. I will be a friend to myself and offer myself the same compassion I would offer to another in my place.

I let go of negative labels, such as lazy or bad or clumsy, that I have used to describe myself these long years, recognizing that labels are inaccurate and destructive and that they stifle growth.

I will refrain from attacking myself with ridicule, disgust, or punishment when I do something that displeases me.

I will absorb rather than deflect the positives others give to me. I realize I need information about myself that will help me choose a positive self-portrait.

Because we are all unique, I refrain from comparing myself to other people, realizing that this is like comparing apples to oranges. Instead, I will compare me to myself.

Focusing inward, I will set personal goals and measure my own growth by gauging the distance I have come since my last measurement.

I realize I have the right to my own feelings, opinions,

beliefs, and values and that I do not have to defend these positions. I will stand for what I believe (feel) (need) rather than alter my position for fear of disapproval.

I will represent myself when others want to make decisions that affect me.

I trust myself to make personal decisions, realizing that decisions are always guesses and that in some cases no decision is perfect. I give myself permission to make "wrong" decisions without exacting penalties from myself. I will be decisive in making decisions that move me ahead rather than immobilizing myself by agonizing over which decision is "right."

I will take risks by changing my behavior to meet ever-changing circumstances rather than clinging to obsolete behavior patterns that offer the security of being familiar.

I will confront my fears and ask myself what is the worst that could happen if my fears were realized. I will then develop a plan to address this potential catastrophe and give myself credit for being able to survive, no matter what.

I release others from the responsibility of making me happy. I take the initiative to get what I need rather than waiting and hoping that somehow what I need will be brought to me by someone else.

I take responsibility for my own feelings and moods, recognizing that I create these emotional states in myself and that I can change them if I choose.

I will share the vulnerable parts of myself with those I love.

I will function as best I can in the here-and-now of my life rather than cling to the misfortunes and tragedies of my past and allow them to interfere with the present.

I choose to be happy now—to celebrate all the small pleasures of life as they occur—instead of putting happiness off until I get married (get divorced) (make my first million) (make my second million) (move) (go to heaven) (and so on).

I commit, as a forever-growing human being, to invest in myself, to pursue my own dreams, and to become all that I am capable of becoming, for my own sake.

Sources

Abeel, Erica. "The Hurting Husband." *Ladies' Home Journal,* January 1981.

Adler, Bill. "What Is a Mother?" *McCall's,* May 1986.

Appelo, Tim. "Welcome to the '90s." *Savvy Woman,* January 1989.

Atkinson, Holly. *Women and Fatigue.* New York: G. P. Putnam's Sons, 1985.

Bepko, Claudia, and Jo-Ann Krestan. "Too Good for Her Own Good?" *New Woman,* June 1990.

Berg, Barbara J. "Working Mother Overload." *Redbook,* March 1989.

Berg, Elizabeth. "Why I'm At Home." *Parents,* April 1987.

Berman, Laura. "Sheer Imperfection." *Self,* August 1989.

Berry, Alice. In "Fair Plays." *Reader's Digest,* January 1981.

Bombeck, Erma. "Time Heals, Laughter Helps." *Redbook,* October 1992.

Braiker, Harriet B. *Getting Up When You Feel Down.* New York: Simon & Schuster, 1988.

Branden, Nathaniel. "The Greatest Love." *New Woman,* August 1993.

Briggs, Dorothy Corkille. *Celebrate Your Self.* Garden City, N.Y.: Doubleday, 1977.

Brody, Jane. *Good Food Book.* New York: Norton Co., 1985.

Brothers, Joyce. *How to Get Whatever You Want Out of Life.* New York: Simon & Schuster, 1978.

Brothers, Joyce. *The Successful Woman.* New York: Simon & Schuster, 1988.

Browder, Sue. "When Your Independence Conflicts with Love." *New Woman,* September 1988.

Caine, Lynn. "Mother Guilt." *New Woman,* May 1985.

Cannon, Elaine, comp. *Notable Quotables from Women to Women.* Salt Lake City: Bookcraft, 1992.

Carrington, Patricia. *Releasing.* New York: William Morrow, 1984.

"Chemical Depression." *Deseret News,* September 2, 1988.

Coudert, Jo. "How to Make More Time for Yourself." *Woman's Day,* March 7, 1989.

Crosby, Betsy Kilday. "The Mommy Wars." *Family Circle,* February 20, 1990.

Dyer, Wayne. *Your Erroneous Zones.* New York: Harper Paperbacks, 1976.

Fasciano, Nancy. "Guilt Trip." *Working Mother,* April 1985.

Fitzpatrick, Jean. "The Dirty Truth About Housework." *Parents,* January 1984.

Foley, Denise. "The Care and Feeding of a Hardworking Woman." *Prevention,* June 1986.

Freedman, Rita. *Beauty Bound.* Lexington, Mass.: Lexington Books, 1986.

Fruedenberger, Herbert J., and Gail North. *Women's Burnout.* Garden City, N.Y.: Doubleday, 1986.

Fury, Kathleen. "Have You Seen Your Wife Lately?" *Working Woman,* November 1989.

Galinsky, Ellen, and Judy David. "Say Goodbye to Guilt." *Family Circle,* September 20, 1988.

Gallagher, Nora. *Simple Pleasures: Wonderful and Wild Things to Do at Home.* Reading, Mass.: Addison-Wesley, 1981.

Garey, Ellen. "How I Rediscovered My Kids." *Parents,* April 1987.

Gillies, Jean, ed. *How to Run Your House Without Letting It Run You.* Garden City, N.Y.: Doubleday, 1973.

Grant, Roberta. "Who's Running Your Life?" *Ladies' Home Journal,* August 1985.

Hagerty, Betty L. In "All in a Day's Work." *Reader's Digest,* August 1982.

Halas, Celia, and Roberta Matteson. *I've Done So Well—Why Do I Feel So Bad?* New York: Ballantine Books, 1978.

Hales, Dianne. "Are You Too Good a Wife?" *Woman's Day,* May 10, 1988.

Hales, Dianne. "You've Done Your Best. Why Do You Still Feel Guilty?" *McCall's,* June 1983.

Hekker, Terry. *Ever Since Adam and Eve.* New York: William Morrow & Co., 1979.

Hochschild, Arlie. *The Second Shift: Working Parents and the Revolution at Home.* New York: Viking Press, 1989.

Hoffecker, Pamela Hobbs. "Will the Real Working Mom Please Stand Up?" *Parents,* April 1985.

Holland, Barbara. "The Phone Is Ringing, a Child Has Just Skinned Its Knee, the Soup Is Boiling Over, the Cat Is Throwing Up and Someone's at the Door: Which Do You Take Care of First?" *McCall's,* July 1983.

Hutchinson, Marcia Germaine. *Transforming Body Image.* Trumansburg, N.Y.: The Crossing Press, 1985.

Jarvik, Elaine. "Victim Breaks Silence on 'Depression After Delivery.'" *Deseret News,* July 7, 1989.

Johnson, Stephen M. *First Person Singular: Living the Good Life Alone.* Philadelphia: Lippincott, 1977.

Kaufman, Margo. "The Perfect Woman." *Working Woman,* October 1991.

Keen, Sam. "Coping with Anxiety and Guilt." *Family Circle,* January 1, 1977.

Krucoff, Carol. "The Chores Wars." *Ladies' Home Journal,* July 1984.

Kubler-Ross, Elisabeth. *Death: The Final Stage of Growth*. Englewood Cliffs, N.J.: Prentice Hall, 1975.

Kubler-Ross, Elisabeth. *On Death and Dying*. New York: Macmillan, 1969.

Langway, Lynn. "The She Decade." *Ladies' Home Journal*, November 1989.

Larmouth, Jeanine. "The Pleasures of Lists." *Reader's Digest*, March 1990.

Larson, Peter J. "Partners in Grime." *Reader's Digest*, September 1992.

Lein, Laura. *Families Without Villains*. Lexington, Mass.: Lexington Books, 1984.

Leinen, Carol. In "Life in These United States." *Reader's Digest*, December 1985.

Lerner, Harriet. *The Dance of Anger*. New York: Harper and Row, 1985.

Leuth, Shirley. "Happy Mother's Day (I Think)." *McCall's*, May 1984.

Libman, Joan. "How Close Are You to Motherhood Burnout?" *Family Circle*, July 2, 1985.

Lippert, Joan. "Life With Brian." *Health*, August 1986.

Livingstone, Isobel L. "Pipe Dreams." *Reader's Digest*, November 1987.

Markowitz, Roberta. "Today's Busy Woman's Biggest Complaint: I'm Too Tired for Sex." *Redbook*, November 1987.

Martino, Virginia. *Reminisce*. Premier Collections Edition, 1992.

Matthews, Sanford, M.D., and Maryann Bucknum Brinley. "The Biggest Mistake a Mother Can Make!" *Redbook*, October 1982.

McBride, Mary. *Don't Call Mommy at Work Today Unless the Sitter Runs Away*. New York: Brothers Grinn, 1992.

McCammon, Anne. "Beating the Blues at Last." *New Woman*, February 1990.

McGinley, Phyllis. *The Providence of the Heart.* New York: Viking Penguin, 1982.

McGrath, Lee Parr. *What Is a Grandmother?* New York: Simon & Schuster, 1970.

McPhedran, Kerry. "Are You Trying Too Hard to Be Perfect?" *New Woman,* July 1985.

Michaels, Marguerite. "Why More Mothers Stay Home." *Family Circle,* October 13, 1985.

Mundis, Hester. *Powermom.* New York: Congdon & Weed, 1984.

Ochs, Vanessa L. "On Being a Classy Mother." *Woman's Day,* May 5, 1987.

Oppenheim, Josie A. "Stay-At-Home Moms." *Good Housekeeping,* September 1990.

Optimist Magazine, February 1990, as quoted in *Reader's Digest,* July 1990.

Orsborn, Carol. *You Don't Have to Be Perfect: Enough Is Enough.* New York: Pocket Books, 1988.

Pittman, Frank. "Not For Men Only: Women's Work??" *New Woman,* July 1991.

Pogrebin, Letty Cottin. "Let's Stop Sweeping the Truth about Housework under the Rug." *Good Housekeeping,* October 1983.

Prose, Francine. "Somehow It's Always My Fault." *Working Mother,* December 1987.

Reilly, William J. "So You Want Money." *New Woman,* October 1983.

Russianoff, Penelope. "Are You Hurt Too Easily?" *Working Mother,* January 1989.

Ruta, Suzanne. "If the Kid Is Sick It's Got to Be My Fault." *Working Mother,* November 1983.

Schaef, Anne Wilson. *Meditations for Women Who Do Too Much.* San Francisco: Harper & Row, 1990.

Schoonmaker, Mary Ellen. "The Jolly Job Market." *Family Circle,* January 9, 1990.

Schulman, Candy. "You Know You're a Mother When . . . " *Family Circle,* May 17, 1988.

"Self Survey." *Self,* September 1989.

Shaevitz, Marjorie Hansen. *The Superwoman Syndrome.* New York: Warner Books, 1984.

Shainess, Natalie. "Are You Too Good for Your Own Good?" *Redbook,* June 1984.

Stechert, Kathryn. "Trying to Be Perfect." *Working Mother,* October 1988.

Stern, Ellen Sue. *The Indispensable Woman.* New York: Bantam Books, 1988.

Stern, Ellen Sue. "The Indispensable Woman." *New Woman,* April 1989.

Strong, Maggie. "More Power to You." *Redbook,* September 1983.

Tannenhauser, Carol. "Motherhood Stress." *Woman's Day,* December 26, 1985.

Thoele, Sue Patton. *The Courage to Be Yourself.* Berkeley, Calif.: Conari Press, 1988.

Thompson, Mary Jane. "If Mothers Could Have All Their Wishes." *McCall's,* May 1989.

van Klompenburg, Carol. *What To Do When You Can't Do It All.* Minneapolis: Augsburg Publishing House, 1989.

Viorst, Judith. "Domestic Tranquillity." *Redbook,* April 1980.

Viorst, Judith. "Why Don't You Stand Up for Yourself?" *Redbook,* April 1988.

Viscott, David. *How to Live with Another Person.* New York: Pocket Books, 1974.

von Hoffman, Nicholas. "American Woman of the '90s." *Self,* January 1990.

Walters, Marianne, and Nonny Wajchrzyk. "When Women Raise Families Alone." *Good Housekeeping,* March 1982.

Weller, Sheila. "One Woman's Family: The Plight of Single Mothers." *McCall's,* February 1989.

Whitman, Ardis. "What Women Won't Trade for 'Independence.'" *Woman's Day,* May 19, 1978.

Wiley, Kim Wright. "Motherhood's No Snap." *Working Mother,* October 1988.

Wilson, Jeanie. "Make Peace with Your Body." *Woman's Day,* June 23, 1992.

Wyse, Lois. "So Long, Supermom." *Good Housekeeping,* November 1981.

Zobel, Allia. "A Toast to Singlehood." *New Woman,* March 1988.